Robert M. Katzman

Fighting Words:

Saul Bellow Kosher Pickles and The Aluminum Fortress

Stories of My Life
Volume III

A Fighting Words Publishing Book

Published and distributed by:
Fighting Words Publishing Company
P. O. Box 7
Highwood, IL 60040
(847) 274-1474
email: bob@fightingwordspubco.com
Website: www.fightingwordspubco.com

This book is dedicated to:

Christine ZumBahlen Shoub
1952 - 2006

Too fine a person, and too essential to my earlier life, for me to just let her slip silently beneath the earth.

Her song must be sung.

Christine's name opens my book, and her story — never meant to be written by me — about the brief intersections of our lives, ends it.

I will never forget her, and my memoir from another time is meant to honor her.

She deserves that.

Her spirit inhabits these pages.

<u>Other books and publications by Robert M. Katzman</u>

Fighting Words: 1965-1985 Chicago's Bob's Newsstand
I'm Not Dead...Yet
Stories of My Life, Volume I

Fighting Words: Escaping and Embracing the Cops of Chicago
Stories of My Life, Volume II

All the Countries of Europe and All the U.S. States
Arranged by Size
(Plus Israel)

<u>Coming Soon!</u>

Fighting Words:
<u>*Hot Sex and Small Change*</u>:
True Confessions of a Teenaged Newsvendor
... and other stories

Robert M. Katzman

Fighting Words: Saul Bellow, Kosher Pickles and
The Aluminum Fortress
Stories of My Life, Volume III

Table of contents

Why Read My Stories?	1
Everyone Needs Heroes	4
1. Saul Bellow, Kosher Pickles and	14
The Aluminum Fortress	
2. An American Classic	94
The Kaage Newsstand	
3. The Thousand Dollar Bill	114
4. The Chocolate Frosting Conspiracy	132
5. Introduction and Insight into A Child's Holocaust Story	146
A Child's Holocaust Story	152
6. A Short Story without a Name	178
7. The Foreclosure Quintet	188
8. Losing Christine	238

Why Read My Stories?

Because some people need a voice to scream their anguish, determination, frustration and independence.

Some people need to know that though life may knock them down again and again, that though they may have lost all that they own and see their future as only a black hopeless emptiness—that they are *not* alone.

The battle is not over until *you* say it's over.

Until *you* want to quit.

It is not for *other* people to decide what you are, who you are and what you are made of.

A person is so much more than where they live, what they wear and what they drive. A person is so much more than *stuff*.

If the whole world says that you are nothing, and never will be anything, but your wife and children see you as the rock of their lives—then you are just that: A Rock.

If the people closest to you—family, true friends—see the real you, your character, your love for them, the good that lives in you—then all the other people's words are just dust.

This book is not about triumph.

It's about *not* accepting failure as your destiny.

Don't quit.

Get up.

Start over.

Believe in yourself.

It is the steel in your spine that matters most, not your paycheck or your lack of one.

I've lost one business after another, gone bankrupt, lost a home.

I've often said that I'm on the cutting edge of obsolescence. Every way of making a living that I've ever tried was just about past its time, just as I plunged into it.

Newspaper stands—gone!

Independent bookstores–gone!

Back issue magazine stores–gone!

I've had twenty-nine operations—from foot surgery to brain surgery, twice—and I'm still here.

I still believe in me.

I still have value.

Someone still needs me.

It's still up to *me* when it's over.
And it's still up to *you*.

My stories are about my defiance against unjust companies, governments, hospitals and prejudice. Stories about standing up to sneering bullies. About standing by my friends, and thank God, their standing by me.

Stories about overcoming oppression, fear and striking back when the time came for me to strike back.

Loves lost and love found.

Finding out that I had real grit and was not just anyone's pawn.

If God gave me the gift of being able to put one word next to another and end up with sentences that say *exactly* what someone else's heart feels and wants and dreams, then I have found the reason for *my* life.

Despite all the pain, loss and humiliation that have rained down on me, all my life—

I *still* believe in me.

Do you still believe in you?

**At Brookfield Zoo with my family in Summer 1986
From the left: Bob, 36, David, 8, Lisa, 11, Irving, 74,
Joy, 36 and Rachel, 6.**

Adele Warman

Everyone Needs Heroes

My Aunt Adele complains that I never write anything about her. My first reaction to her was: Have you read all my stories? You should be grateful you are *not* someone I'm trying to recover from. But then, you're a Galitzianer, so I guess I have to make allowances for you. But do you really want to keep company with:

Those two violent cops that beat me up one dark night, by mistake. My crazed mother, ditto. Or a killer winter blizzard that trapped my family in North Dakota for twelve terrifying hours. Or some girl(s) that abandoned me and broke my heart. Or some incompetent surgeon that was learning on the job, with me. Or some low-life from Chicago's City Hall out to shake me down, threatening to tear apart my newsstand. Or some *Twinkie* on the nightshift that refused to give me a pain pill, when I was in intensive care after a transplant operation.

Or that idiot art teacher from my eighth grade that had me suspended from my grammar school for three days because she didn't like how I wanted to draw a picture. Or those three schmucks in my freshman high school French class that didn't like my nose and reminded me about it, daily, for months. Or that drunken giant in the Tennessee strip joint that wanted to kill me because he thought I stole a dollar from him.

Not being written about, Aunt Adele, could reasonably be considered an *honor* if you stop to consider the charming cast of characters above that I *did* choose to immortalize. You just weren't horrible enough to make the cut, I guess.

Not only weren't you horrible enough to cause me more pain, but you were the closest thing I had for a *real* mother, a loving mother, for the first fourteen years of my life. Not only weren't you crazy, but you hugged me **so** tightly, whenever I saw you, I thought my spine would snap. No distant, arms-length love from you. Not a chance of that.

Am I supposed to complain that you would cook anything I could possibly want, as long as it consisted of peanut butter and jelly? And Silvercup white bread? Should I have to remember that you constantly told strangers how clever I was, or funny, or whatever nice thing you could think of to say that no one else ever said about me? Why should I want to remember something insignificant like that?

Never write about you? What about the dozens of poems specifically written just for you, in that box under your bed?

When I first met you, April 30 1950, when I was born, and you were almost seventeen, you were still simply Adele Warman, before you married everybody on the South Side of Chicago, sequentially. Somehow, to me, you still seem to be my teenaged aunt, even into your seventies...the one that played all that very loud rock 'n roll music, while I was still teething. Sometimes I mix you up with Peggy Sue...

**Adele, in 1975, with her daughters:
Diana, left and Julie, right.**

Adele, on her wedding day. Truly a beautiful bride!
Back row, from left: Her sister and Matron of Honor, Anne
Warman Katzman (my mother); her new mother-in-law, Mary
Galai; her sister-in-law and a bridesmaid, Shyrl Warman (my
aunt); her mother, Celia Warman (my grandmother); two
bridesmaids and friends, Nancy Stotland and Teri Cole. The
two young girls in front are her nieces: left, Caryn Warman,
flower girl (my cousin) and right, Bonnie Sue Katzman,
junior bridesmaid (my sister).

Anne Warman, 20, with her little sister, Adele, 8.

So, you want me to write something about you? Okay, but remember, you asked for it. Try this item on for size:

In December 1968, when I was just out of intensive care, after my cancer surgery, and I had new steel rods in my face where my left jaw used to be, you came to visit me in the hospital. I was just eighteen, very weak, in continuous pain and my face was swathed in thick pads and bandages like I was the mummy from some horror movie. I felt so miserable and so sorry for myself that *nobody* could do *anything* to change my mood.

You dramatically pulled back the curtain around my bed and stood there staring at me—with that mock serious expression you always seemed to have—waiting for me to say something funny. You always thought I was *so* funny. The fact that this was probably the most miserable moment of my young life did not stop you from expecting me to perform on cue. No sir, not you.

But then, inexplicably inspired by your presence, I held up my IV tube and pointed up to the glucose bag hanging from the tall metal pole next to my bed and said to you sternly, through my muffling bandages:

"Adele, I can't talk to you now...can't you see I'm eating?"

Well, you just about fell over in hysterics, like I was all the clowns in the Barnum and Bailey Circus, rolled into one. Your just being there, standing silently at the foot of my bed, was enough to take my mind off all my self-pity and force me to be who I really was, if only for a moment. A very good moment. Only you could do that.

So why in the world should I write anything about you? Are you so special?

Yeah, you are.

I guess you'll have to settle for remaining on that ivory pedestal I keep you on, held up there by my rock-solid love for you, for the rest of your life. And mine, too.

So, I'm sorry, Aunt Adele.

There's really nothing else for me to say.

****

To my **Secret Ally Within The Charles Levy Circulating Company**, during the savage and virtually hopeless **Magazine Wars**, 1976-1980:

You know what you did, you know why you did it, and you know what it meant to me and my family. Despite my eventual and unavoidable fate as the bitter consequence of taking on such an overwhelming opponent, I have no regrets. Although it has been many years since we last saw each other, I hope you are still alive, healthy and that you finally found the elusive true love you were looking for.

Your brave act, on my company's behalf, at last proved our case and brought that long battle to a close. It also tested my character, and courage, in a way I never would have been able to know for sure, without the uproar your secret communication caused.

Despite our earlier differences that caused pain to both of us, I have always felt love and gratitude toward you. Always.

Maybe you'll see this public note to you in a bookstore, some day. Maybe you'll contact me and let me know how the last twenty-five years have treated you. I sure hope so, my friend. I'd like you to meet my beautiful new daughter, Sarah, who is now ten. The last time you saw my oldest daughter, Lisa, she was about three, during Halloween, when we bobbed for apples. Now Lisa is married and thirty-two years old. Maybe you'll have someone you'll want me to meet, as well.

Then I can tell that person what a brave person you were, an Army of One, riding to rescue me during a very dark hour of my life. I will never forget you and what your decision to join the fight meant to me.

Call me some time and we can talk about it over coffee. I'd sure like that, my old friend. Until then, your secret identity will remain safe, deep within me.

Love, Bob

****

****

Marshal Morris, aka Marshall Marshall, has ridden his Appaloosa into my life in the Prairie State on two occasions: In 1987 and again in 2005. Unlike Jimmy Stewart in *The Man Who Shot Liberty Valance*, where Stewart played a civilized, peaceable lawyer out of the East, and who firmly believed that the law must prevail over mindless violence, Marshall Marshall's unique attitude is:

"If we lose the damn case, I'm gonna shoot that son-of-a-bitch right in the nuts!"

Okay, he never said that. But in reality, he definitely saved my ass in two quite desperate situations, neither of which involved gunplay. I first met him when, after a major loss in an earlier case in court, I turned for help to a lawyer in my family who listened to my grief, and then recommended Marshal.

"Why him," I asked my cousin, "instead of any of a hundred other lawyers?"

"Because," he replied, matter-of-factly, "when a guy's situation is so totally loused up beyond any possible chance of redeeming his case, Morris is the only guy I know who—positively—can turn things around for you and keep your ass out of jail."

And, that is exactly how things turned out for me. If I had to choose between a .357 Magnum and a legal mouthpiece like Marshal Morris for protection, there'd be no contest, Pilgrim. Morris' brain is more like a Howitzer.

Well, I better mosey along now...I gotta meet a guy at some place called The OK Corral. You ever heard about some skinny dentist named...**Doc Holliday?**

****

"If we lose the damn case, I'm gonna shoot that son-of-a-bitch right in the nuts!"

Authors note: The words above were not exactly stated by my esteemed legal representative, but rather, are intended to capture the wild 'n wooly independent western spirit of the man. I found him to be a real straight-shooter... RMK

Saul Bellow Chapter Headings

I - Scratching for a Buck; A Chance Meeting;
I Discover the High School Newspaper

◆

II - The Alien World of New York Times Readers
To a Kid from Chicago's South Side
My First Newsstand Opens

◆

III - Prisoner of My Newsstand: It Burns;
It Burns Again, but I Still Remain Its Captive

◆

IV - My 53rd Street Newsstand Burns and
Becomes the Aluminum Fortress

◆

V - Loyalty, Corruption and The Chicago Machine

◆

VI - My Kosher Delicatessen Opens
Hyde Park Learns to Love Lox Between
Two Pieces of Newsprint

◆

VII - My Dad, A Tough West Side Jew
Class Begins: Chicago 101

VIII - *Chicago 102: Payoffs*
Learning to Survive in Corrupt Chicago

◆

IX - *The Kosher Mouse*
Forty Years Later, I'm Still not Taking His Calls

◆

X - *My Break with My Uncle Ziggy —*
Defeated, I Leave the Deli

◆

XI - *Paying Dad's Debts with Kosher Pickles*

◆

XII - *Mish-Mash*
Corned Beef with Ketchup, France, Mustard
and Other Problems

◆

XIII - *Saul Bellow Returns: My Gulliver's Bookstore Opens*

◆

XIV - *Where Do Books Go when a Bookstore Dies?*

◆

XV - *About Those Books…*

◆

XVI - *Good-bye to Saul Bellow*
(Possibly) One Last Crossing of Our Paths

Saul Bellow

1

Saul Bellow, Kosher Pickles and The Aluminum Fortress

Part I:
Scratching for a Buck; A Chance Meeting; I Discover the High School Newspaper

When I was in high school, in 1964—specifically the University of Chicago Laboratory High School, or Lab School as it was commonly known—the famous author, Saul Bellow, and his many paperback novels were frequently seen in the library, or in the English Department on someone's desk, or else assigned to us to be read by an admiring teacher.

Once there was a display of six of his books in a glass case on the wall in a major hallway for months, celebrating the U.of C.'s very popular local writer.

I'd never read him.

I was working seven days a week to pay for that very expensive school, and when I tried to read any book at night, I'd inevitably fall immediately asleep. I had long known his name, and was aware that he was a literary hero in the Jewish community and very respected by the Hyde Park intelligentsia, in general. I also knew what he looked like: snow white hair combed over to the side, kind of droopy, baggy eyes, and a wide smile with a large lower lip, on a pale, world-weary face.

Like most famous people, he may as well have been President Johnson, for all the likelihood that I would ever meet him. His circles were not my circles. I wasn't the child of a critic, or playwright, or a publisher. While many Lab School parents were very well off or socially prominent in Chicago or beyond, my dad, at the moment, sold life insurance. We scraped by, and we were unlikely to run into Mr. Bellow at a University cocktail party.

The very idea that I would ever write a book of my own, about myself, of all topics, was way beyond a remote possibility. But life in my case has been far better than fiction, and I did meet Saul Bellow several times, in different situations, and I'm still not wealthy or socially prominent.

So, there!

I had already been writing poetry since I was eight years old, so it made sense to me when I was a high school junior, in 1966, to join the staff of the Lab School newspaper, *The Midway*, especially after I learned that being on the newspaper allowed you to wander the halls, at any time, without a signed permission slip.

I was never thrilled at the prospect of some officious prick of a hall guard cross-examining me on my reasons for going here or there. Actually, I wasn't too keen on asking anyone's permission for any reason whatsoever, so working on the school paper was perfect.

I didn't anticipate that our journalism teacher, a young Mr. Wayne Brasler, who would be commonly considered by his peers around the country, in the years to come, to be one of the best in his field in the United States, and much honored, would be such a compelling role model for me. Nor did I ever expect the quality of my stories to rise to his very high standards and to actually become an incisive, persistent and concise reporter and writer.

Also a columnist, photographer, cartoonist, advertisement designer and salesman.

There was even an extended period when I was asked to write for the Parent-Teacher Newsletter, after I wrote a column where I interviewed the assistant principal and good-naturedly compared him to a chipmunk.

The Newsletter editor was aghast at this apparently cheeky insult, but also amused because the little guy really did resemble a chipmunk, and she actually ran the interview, intact. We waited apprehensively for the fallout; but to our mutual amazement, suddenly the editor began receiving all these calls from other faculty members demanding to be interviewed and compared to other equally interesting wildlife! I did a few more interviews to a pretty good reception, and then decided to get out before the "animals" became restless.

I became very good, very confident at all of these things, whereas before going under the wing of Wayne Brasler, still my friend today after thirty-six years, I'd always felt that I wasn't very much good at anything, except fighting, disrupting classes and in general, antagonizing people.

I even got suspended from Hebrew School one time for, well, gambling and fighting in the hallways. Up until then, I didn't think they could do that. Did that mean I was, God forbid, momentarily Christian until the suspension was removed? Jesus, Joseph and Mary!

Wayne Brasler was exacting, intolerant of slipshod work and

Kat Knips

She's woman of few words, he's of a heady profession

Amid "Humbolt's Guide to the Himalayas" and "The Disturbed Child" stands a petite woman who says three words: "And?" "Thank-you," and "next!"

Along with Bookstore Manager Charles Urbanas, Miss E. Clute ("E. will be sufficient, young man," she said firmly), daily faces unruly, noisy masses of U-Highers as she mans the bookstore in Belfield.

Robert Katzman

A COMPACT PACKAGE of energy and efficiency, Miss Clute came to the bookstore from Marshall, Michigan (where she was born and reared), after a few intermediate jobs. She didn't specify.

"Young students needn't know every detail of my personal life," she asserted.

But Marshall and Chicago are not the only places Miss Clute has been. She's taken trips to Hawaii and the Mediterranean.

MR. URBANAS, who formerly dwelled in the heady profession of rare book collecting and buying, believes people don't accumulate books anymore.

"It used to be," he reflected, "when you went into a person's home, whole walls would be covered with four, five hundred books. Maybe a thousand. Now people think books clash with the design of their houses."

GIVING BOOK-BUYING up after his employer retired seven years ago, Mr. Urbanas came to U-High.

"The curriculum at this school is on a very high plane," he asserted. "The books we sell here usually surprise visitors from other schools."

Miss Clute becomes nettled by dawdlers and smart alecks in the bookstore.

"Kids who run in and say 'this is a stickup'; they interrupt the efficiency of the store," grumbled Miss Clute.

"All we want is to run an efficient shop," she sighed.

• • •

The students at Carl Sandburg high in Orland Park refer to themselves as "Sand Burgers."

Meow, cats.

PAGE TWO—TUESDAY, JANUARY 30, 1968

I wrote a column for *The Midway* called "Kat Knips," and sketched many of the paper's cartoons, which were usually political in nature.

'What we need is a standard dress code'

Above: A *U-High Midway* staff meeting. I'm on the left.
Below: My journalism teacher, Wayne Brasler.

demanded that deadlines be met, no exceptions. That news reports were to be clear, to the point, correct and easy to shorten as space demands required; meaning that all the pertinent facts had to be in the first paragraph. He treated words as drops of gold, not to be squandered; but he edited with an ax.

"Too wordy!" he'd bellow, so that the whole class—eight people—could witness your incompetence. *"Cut it down! Cut it down! Get to the essence of the story!"* he'd demand.

I am more than twice as old now as Wayne was then, in 1966 (twenty-five), and I am about the same age today as Saul Bellow was at that time, by coincidence. Mr. Bellow was born in 1915 in Quebec, Canada, and as of this writing in 2002, he still lives, at eighty-seven years old.

But my journalism class was still in the future, in this story.

In the summer of 1964, I was a cashier and general slave at the corner drug store near where I lived with my father, about two blocks south of the Museum of Science and Industry, at Lake Michigan and 57th Street, in Hyde Park.

In addition to selling condoms—one at a time, over the counter—ice cream, candy and cigarettes, I also delivered prescriptions to people, using the drug store's rusty, rickety bicycle. Despite lurid stories told to me by older employees, no sexy woman ever came to the door in her underwear, or less, to receive her prescriptions from the eager delivery boy, and then seductively try to entice me in. All the people I delivered to were fat, bald, old, sick people—crabby, impatient and unhappy. Some, most, didn't tip.

One notable exception to the old, crabby, etc. rule was Saul Bellow, who had the flu, I guess, and came to the door in his bathrobe, smiling, friendly and courteous. Soft-spoken and charming with kind eyes, he accepted his medicine, thanked me and even included a tip. That was my first contact with Saul Bellow—when I was fourteen.

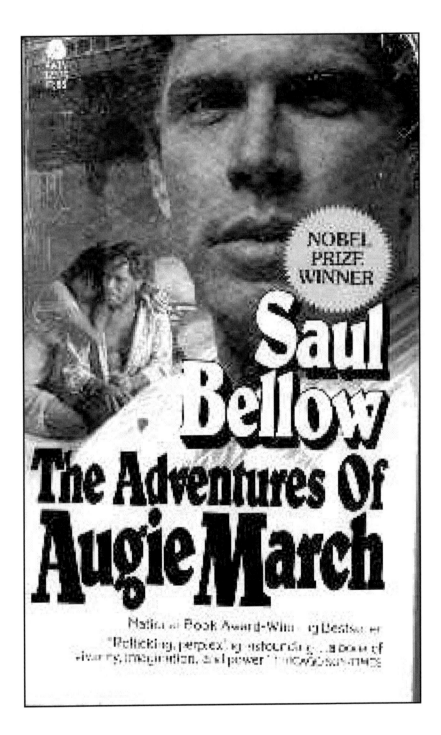

Part II:
The Alien World of the *New York Times* Readers to a South Side of Chicago Kid: My Newsstand Opens

A year later, in 1965, I opened what was to be a very popular newspaper stand in Hyde Park, at 51st Street and Lake Park Avenue, a key transit corner by the train, many bus stops, a cab stand and a future shopping center. I would remain connected to that corner, despite numerous other adventures and enterprises, for the next twenty years.

I sold the *New York Times*, among many other items, and in Hyde Park, anyone with any interest in international politics, world financial conditions, the latest reviews of notable art galleries, movies—domestic and foreign—plays, books, fashion, and obscure, but worthy restaurants in Chelsea, Christopher Street, Greenwich Village or over on Delancy Street, read the *New York Times*.

At its peak, my newsstand sold one thousand *New York Times* every Sunday morning—a logistical nightmare that required an army of reluctant kids to help assemble the four to five thousand components that made up the *Times* Sunday edition; and that paper didn't even have any color comic section! But the women's lingerie ads kind of made up for that, at least in my opinion.

We'd start work at five a.m., driving down to Union Station in central Chicago to pick up the lead-heavy bundles, tied with thick wire, where they were stacked in a mountain of newspapers, waiting for my crew and I to transfer them, by hand, from the cold concrete dock to my huge, old truck—big as a moving van. We packed the bundles tightly, floor to ceiling, front to back, then drove back to the newsstand very slowly, the ancient transmission crying all the way.

The *New York Times* was the essential key to my newsstand's initial popularity because my customers would not only stop to buy their "Holy East Coast Bible," but also shop for other magazines at the same time. Not every newsvendor could get the *Times* from the local distributor, and I was very determined not to lose any customers because of a late delivery or disorganization.

I used to hang a sign up on the outside of my newsstand's overhanging wooden roof to notify the Sunday morning army of ravenous, culture hungry *Times* customers whether or not the newspaper had arrived and was available for purchase. In the early morning hours, we were positively besieged by extremely impatient *Times* customers who wanted to get going with their Sunday morning plans for the day, but would not even *consider* going to their favorite restaurant for brunch, fresh-squeezed orange juice and cappuccino without that precious five pounds of newsprint clutched firmly in their arms.

They distained the local Chicago newspapers as so much illiterate trash, and would never consider any of them as alternatives if the *Times* was late.

The signs—there were two of them—said simply:

"not yet" and "it's in"

I thought this was a very uncomplicated and direct way to communicate with my customers and save endless conversations. People could see the signs as they drove by or as far as a block away if they were on foot.

I did *NOT* see the possibly lurid connotations or other interpretations some people might perceive from these simple, hand-painted black and white signs hanging from the metal eye-hooks screwed into my roof, swaying slightly in the breeze.

But some clever journalistic types apparently thought these signs were hysterical, blatantly sexual, and in one of the initial editions of an early *Chicago City Magazine*, they ran a picture of an impishly smiling teenaged me, framed in the little sales window of the newsstand holding the **"it's in!"** sign so it rested on the window sill.

They seemed very smug and pleased with themselves that they had discovered this hidden innuendo that some clueless paperboy was oblivious to, and must have felt that they were very sophisticated urban recorders of the bizarre and exotic city scene. But no one else must have shared their high opinion of themselves, or their unique sense of humor, and the magazine folded after just a few issues.

"It's in!"

"Not yet."

I once read that if a woman has to ask you: **"Is it in yet?"** you were already in serious trouble. But that's another story, and fortunately, I'm not in it.

At least…not yet.

On one memorable occasion, my large truck was being repaired and the only rental van that was available on short notice was, regrettably, too small for such a heavy load of newspaper bundles.

Soon after leaving Union Station and almost immediately after entering the interstate highway to get back to the newsstand, our left rear tire blew completely off its rim. The van began swerving, but I quickly slowed way down to twenty miles an hour. We continued on that way, riding on three tires and a rapidly deforming rim, for the last five miles, hoping, praying, that no cops would notice our crawling, tilting van and force us off the interstate.

None did, and we finally made it back to the newsstand, an hour late, and encountered an antagonized, impatient crowd of *Times* customers surrounding the stand. It felt like we were the cavalry, rescuing the wagon train surrounded by hostiles.

Swiftly setting up an on-the-spot assembly line, right on the street, behind the van, instead of inside of it, as usual, I began selling the papers as fast as they were assembled to the milling hoard of intellectuals quite willing to spear me with stinging invective.

Well, one thing I *can* do, after so many years handling rush hours at the newsstand, is to make change really fast. With a blizzard of dollars bills swirling round me, I knocked off the crowd of over fifty snarling people within fifteen minutes of arriving.

There was a somewhat positive end to this bizarre incident. When I returned the van to the rental place, with its ruined left rear rim, I raised hell about the poor quality of their tires, how all our lives had been endangered, and what kind of a candy-ass operation were they running there, anyway? All this ranting with a very straight face.

The manager was overcome with regret and embarrassment at my unfortunate circumstances, especially since there were other customers standing in line behind me. He quickly scrawled "NO

CHARGE" across my rental contract, refunded my deposit and I got the hell out of there.

Among my thousands of customers, including the president of the University of Chicago, doctors, lawyers, Operation Push civil rights leaders, TV personalities, and every rabbi and minister in Hyde Park, it seemed, was Saul Bellow, who like so many others with similar tastes or values, regularly bought the *New York Times*.

But he was never impatient (perhaps he sold newspapers as a boy in Quebec), he was very friendly, and after a while, since I always took care of him myself whenever he happened to stop by for a newspaper, he came to recognize me and knew my name—Bob.

However this was no big deal, because my name was pretty easy to spot since it was a ten-foot long sign attached to the top of the newsstand saying: **"Bob's Newsstand."** At my father's urging, to personalize my newsstand from hundreds of others that existed at the time, I made the sign in shop class in high school, carving out the thirteen capital letters from one ten-foot long plank twelve inches high.

Now if it had been called *"Ezequiel's Newsstand"* or *"Jedediah's Newsstand,"* it might not have penetrated the general consciousness of Hyde Park and Chicago. But "Bob's was pretty easy to remember, and just like that famous bar, "Cheers" on TV, after a while, everybody knew my name.

So that was my second, periodic meeting with Saul Bellow, in 1968, when I was eighteen.

Part III:
A Prisoner of My Newsstand: It Burns;
It Burns Again, but I Remain Its Captive

More time passed, and in 1975, after working at the newsstand for ten years, I was bored and itchy to do something else.

I didn't know what.

Just something.

All my classmates from Lab School were through with college, since the Viet Nam War was finally over, which probably had been a major motivator to many of them to stay in school. Now, some were in graduate school, law school—there ended up being many lawyers, big surprise, including the U. of C.'s President Levi's son, who ended up a federal judge; medical school—we had at least one brain surgeon; and traveling—at least one classmate is still in Japan, thirty years later, and has informed the rest of us through an alumni magazine that he has no intentions of ever returning, and has bought a gravesite, there, to be buried in, some day.

I was still stuck on my corner, selling newspapers to cars.

Now, granted, I sold *a lot* of newspapers, and carried hundreds of domestic and foreign magazines, and was prosperous in general, I guess. I'd been married for four years to a beautiful girl, Barbara, also from the Lab School, Class of '70, and my life was just percolating along.

Aside from about two and a half years of college, at the University of Illinois, Roosevelt, and the U. of C.'s Downtown Extension, I had gone nowhere with higher education, and my long ago dreams of becoming a lawyer were so covered by dust and circumstances, that I never even mourned that lost career anymore.

That is, unless some worldly former classmate came by, while on a visit to Chicago, to see if Ol' Bob was still there, selling newspapers and racing forms at 51st and Lake Park. These visits happened frequently. They wanted to see the eccentric kid that worked his way through one of the most expensive and respected high schools in the United States, and *now* was a real whiz at making change, and snapping the *Final Markets Chicago Daily News* swiftly under your arm, folding it crisply with one hand.

I was twenty-five, finally an adult, and I had begun to feel like one. I wanted some excitement. A new challenge.

My theory of aging at that time was, you didn't really grow and mature at a constant rate. I felt like I was eighteen for a long time, even though I married at twenty-one. Despite having ten employees and a growing, profitable business, my own self-image lingered on as a slender, medium height kid who just barely graduated high school because of the unusual kindness of the Math Department, and was rough and ready for any adventure. This self-image of my identity dominated my consciousness, despite reality.

At twenty-five, I'd already had numerous major operations, including two unsuccessful transplant attempts to reconstruct my face after cancer surgery at eighteen, where the surgeons removed most of my left jaw—and, as more than a little psychic compensation, kept me out of the Viet Nam War—two hernias and numerous other procedures.

I'd seen my original and largest newsstand burn down twice, in a fiery blink. The first time, November 28, 1970, an eighty year-old, lovable part-time worker, Morris, was trying to keep warm one night while I was catching a few hours sleep. We had an old black kerosene heater, about thirty inches high, that could very effectively roast your nuts as you snuggled close as you dared on arctic winter nights, while at the same time letting your ass freeze crystal blue.

That smoky old heater could positively hypnotize you with its warming lethal gases that flowed freely out of the circle of holes punched out of the top of the heater, especially if you kind of leaned over the top a bit to take the chill out of your poor little nose, and ears and cheeks. We used to cook little cocktail hot dogs over those hot black holes, until a kindly construction worker with extensive experience working outside with those dependable miniature furnaces informed us that we were poisoning ourselves.

Boy, I sure miss those yummy, juicy, kerosene-flavored hot dogs!

Well, one very cold winter night, a semi-alert old Morris was embracing our metal mother when a car pulled up and honked its horn to summon him out to bring it a newspaper. The loud blare of the horn startled Morris out of his sleepy reveries, probably remembering his long ago romances while stationed in France during World War One, the Great War, as it was called, at first.

Morris lurched forward, abruptly, to answer the horn's demands, when his bulky overcoat snagged the handle of the heater as he shuffled out the side door of that very dry, newspaper-filled wooden newsstand, pulling the heater over, exposing its flames to the perfect kindling surrounding it, and that sole source of my support went up like a roaring Roman candle.

Morris was not hurt at all, but one of my two dogs that kept us company while we worked out there at night was burned to death. The dog's name was Hymie, a black and white puppy that a friendly customer donated to the newsstand. I'd like to tell you a couple of sweet, funny stories about that cuddly, lovable dog, but, well, I just can't do it. It still hurts me, thirty years later.

The second fire's circumstances were almost identical to the first one, except that I had switched from a kerosene to an electric heater after I was able to get an electrical hook-up from a nearby street light pole, but only after bribing the appropriate ward politician.

Except *this* time, four years later, in Spring 1974, the unharmed, remorseful employee was eleven years old, which only proves that there are some situations where no matter how you reconfigure significant components in a given situation, you will still inevitably end up with a smoking pile of warm ashes, in the folk wisdom of newspaper stands.

I distinctly remember digging up an old, charred canvas change belt, full of burned pennies, out of the debris, that I washed repeatedly by hand to make them separate and to make the stink go away.

You might doubt anyone would ever be so desperate to bother doing such a thing; but I lost all means of earning a living in that second fire, and after a couple of friends and a relative loaned me enough cash to buy fresh lumber to rebuild the newsstand quickly before it snowed again. I also salvaged as many eight and ten-penny nails as I could, out of the burned two-by-fours, before disposing of all the wreckage, and reused them in building the new structure.

You never know what you'll be willing, or forced to do, until life thrusts a situation upon you, and your free labor and determination to start over again are the only assets you have to resurrect yourself.

An eighty year-old lovable part-time worker, Morris.

hyde park herald wednesday, december 9, 1970 page 3

Photos by Eric Anderson

Firemen try to stifle fire at Bob's newsstand.

Bob to replace burned-out stand

Bob Katzman, whose newsstand at 51st and Lake Park burned last Saturday, will open the "most beautiful newsstand in the world" at the same location.

An electrical fire destroyed Katzman's west stand and "a couple of thousand dollars' worth" of magazines at about 6 p.m. on Nov. 28. Katzman was especially disturbed by the loss of his dog, Hymie, in the flash fire. "She was a puppy, just one month pregnant," he said "I picked her up in the street about six months ago."

Except for the night of the fire, business has continued uninterrupted. It is being conducted at the west stand out of milk cartons. "Bob's East," which distributes the Sunday New York Times among the earliest in the city, has been unaffected. Katzman has been building his new stand with the help of "a Norwegian carpenter." He expects to open sometime this week.

The new stand, he said, will feature "the most diverse collection of magazines and newspapers in Hyde Park.

Part IV:
53rd Street Newsstand Burns:
Becomes The Aluminum Fortress

I'd expanded my business south to two other good corners, so that in Hyde Park it was difficult to buy a newspaper on the main North-South artery, Lake Park Avenue, from someone else but me.

My ownership of the other two newsstands at 53rd and 55th Streets was not generally known, at first. I mean, the *Wall Street Journal* didn't cover the steady expansion of Bob's Newsstands as if it had national importance. Who would care? To the general public, people who ran newsstands were an anachronistic holdover from another era when street urchins would stand on busy corners and scream:

"READ ALL ABOUT IT!"
"CAPONE MOB BOMBS TEMPERANCE MEETING!"

and then they'd sell armfuls of large, single sheet newspapers to impatient buyers, for a penny each.

By 1965, when I started, newspaper stands on corners were largely run by quite old men, in their seventies or more, or their wives, and frequently one or the other was disabled. So many people were subscribing or getting their news from the radio or television, and I'm sure that a significant percentage of the customers of those people felt their patronage was a kind of charity.

Corner by corner, block by block, as those older people became too ill or aged to continue, or just couldn't stand the prospect and hardship of another bitter cold Chicago winter, they found that there was simply no one to sell their forty-year old business to, and they closed up and lived, barely, on social security.

Fifteen year-old Jewish boys from middle-class families on the South Side of Chicago were not lining up to create newsstand empires, so I was pretty much a curiosity—I still am—to the university community. While it may appear humorous for me to kind of ridicule my own importance in the business world by suggesting that *no* established financial publication would *ever* give a damn what I ever did on any given day, by the end of my twenty-year career running a chain of international newspaper and magazine stores that were so comprehensive in their inventories of special interest periodicals, and so integrated into the fabric of Chicago as essential and dependable sources of exotic information, that not only did my stores receive regular and positive coverage by the local press and television, but my last store's demise was covered, and mourned, by **Crain's Chicago Business**, as perhaps the end of an era.

It was.

But that's all later on in this tale of a young man's progress. So, to return to the past, when an annoyed customer felt our curb service at the 51st Street newsstand was too slow for their impatient schedules, and yelled at me,

"I think I'll take my business to 53rd Street. They're quicker than you guys!"

I would just smile and wave to them as they drove off.

Sometimes I would hitch a ride with a friendly customer while carrying a stack of fifty *Sun-Times* or *Chicago Tribunes* up to the 53rd Street newsstand, and then walk back to the main stand at 51st and Lake Park. I called this the "Lake Park Express," and it only went one way.

Very early, one dark Sunday morning in 1972, a local intoxicated vagrant trying to light his cigarette accidentally set fire to the huge pile of Sunday supplement bundles stacked up against the side wall of the stand at 53rd Street. This wooden newsstand, which I designed myself to match the unusual triangular shape of my officially allotted corner space, was about eighteen feet long in back, ten feet long on each of the two sides, and six feet wide in front. The front, where the little sales window was located, about three feet wide and two feet high, was totally surrounded by current mass-market magazines.

There was a long, low shelf of thick worn wood below the window to hold all the stacks of the various newspapers I carried every day. There were also two heavy, folded wooden doors used to close up the front securely each night, and a steel garage-type unrolling door to lock up the window, so as to protect the valuable magazine inventory inside, in case anyone somehow got past the locked wooden front doors.

You'd think it was a Swiss bank, the way I locked up that little wooden structure every night; but bad guys knocked over newsstands all the time, like tasty appetizers, just before they held up a liquor store.

I arrived at the stand in minutes, after a call from a local cop who knew my number and looked out for me, and I watched dumbly as the flames shot up, in the black nighttime sky, from the wire-bound newspaper bundles, chewing up the wooden wall they were leaning against like it was peanut brittle.

The local fire department trucks were there, as well, and a group of sturdy firefighters quickly pushed the blazing mound of burning Sunday comic sections and Sears ads into the street—almost like a wall of fiery lava pouring over the curb—and as thee bundles crashed into the street, they released a million twinkling sparks, like suicidal fireflies, into the cold, black, night sky.

Then the firemen, coming at the bundles from two sides, drenched the flames, water gushing with enormous pressure from two thick yellow hoses that seemed like huge pythons slithering through the glistening black streets. As the flames died, the many bundles, still tightly bound with strong metal wires, swelled grotesquely like pieces of a broken Michelin Man, lying everywhere in the street.

When those same fireman turned their attention to the newsstand itself, I intervened, and put myself between their powerful hoses and the smoldering wooden wall. I said,

"I'll handle this part, guys, thank you very much."

They looked at me like I was stealing their passes to the Great America Theme Park, but they held back. I knew most of them anyway, from their frequent visits to my 51st Street newsstand to check out the ladies in the latest *Playboy, Penthouse*, or *Juggs-DD*, in the years before the female firefighters got those lovely centerfolds banned from all of America's firehouses.

I knew that the pressure from their hoses was enough to collapse the damaged wooden newsstand, and I felt I could still save it, if only they would let me.

A quick conference with the cops, the fire chief, and myself ensued, with me urgently pleading for a chance to save the little structure, since I was afraid I would not have the money to rebuild it, after two similar recent losses.

These were nice guys, hardworking local guys, that made their living in the streets, like me. After a moment to consider the risk, and knowing how handy I was with hand tools, they agreed to give me two days to make that smoking newsstand safe, or they'd have to knock it down.

They may have been bending the rules about when a fire is officially struck; but there were no flames present, and the very real economic consequences to me were quite clear to those men. Hyde Park was like a little village—a smart little village with a world-class university in it—but an intimate community, nevertheless, where many of the local residents knew each other and the local shopkeepers.

If it had been a Walgreen's Drugstore, or some other major enterprise that had been burning, there'd be no negotiating about anything. The firemen would put out the fire, and the employees would be paid by either the parent company, or their insurance provider.

But when you run a newspaper stand, no matter how neat and clean you and your shack are, or how bustling with customers, there was a general understanding, at least among the men I knew: cab drivers, truck drivers, ambulance drivers and restaurant employees— all hard-working people with lousy, impossible hours—that nobody would work outside all day, in whatever weather, at a newsstand unless there were absolutely no other options.

So the cops, who saw me as an extra pair of eyes on the street, on their side, if they needed me to report if I saw this or that happen, or performing the additional service of giving a lost person directions or some other small assistance, and the firemen, who were mostly close to me in age and very friendly, were more inclined to cut me some slack if it meant keeping me in business. Because, God knows, there sure wasn't any insurance company interested in me.

With the clock now ticking, I opened the door and window, aired out the interior, threw out any damaged merchandise and checked every inch inside, looking in the smoky darkness for any possible remaining spark.

The firemen's initial blasts of water on the burning bundles, while they were still stacked up next to the stand, had soaked and saved the exterior walls, before they shoved the burning bundles into the street. Even so, there was significant superficial damage to repair.

Saul Bellow, in case you were wondering, was not involved in this matter in any way, had nothing to do with the fire, would probably have formed a bucket-brigade to help me if he was anywhere nearby, then written about it in a novel from the Jewish angle, linking burning newsstands with burning books, calling it:

"Where There's Smoke…There's Nazis!"

and then win a Pulitzer Prize for it, go to Washington and meet President Nixon.

What would I get out of all this?

Bubkiss!

Nothing!

Well, Saul Bellow, you can keep your fancy bucket-brigade, thank you very much. I can handle my own newspaper disasters, myself.

And write about them, too!

Seriously, I am obviously kidding about Saul Bellow. I just didn't want him to get lost in all this smoke! I'll get back to him soon, in 1975.

But first, the ultimate defense of my 53rd and Lake Park Newsstand against vagrant firebugs. Determined to not let this combustible situation continue to plague me, I formed a plan that would thwart any future mischief.

I went to a local scrap metal yard at 63rd and State Street and managed to locate a large, tall, roll of industrial aluminum sheeting, big enough to cover the exterior of the newsstand, if I could only unroll it.

Aha!

The Rub!

The price was good, the metal plentiful, but the unrolling was nearly impossible. I smacked the son-of-a-bitch with hammers, jumped on it, cursed the ground it lay on and hit it again with a sledgehammer.

Finally, I got one long edge flattened enough to nail it up along one side of the newsstand, and then was able to use that secured end as an anchor, while I relentlessly beat on the white metal in a seemingly endless effort to flatten out more of the huge roll.

I worked on the mass of metal for hours. I wasn't going to quit, and then I hit upon a scheme that could work: I had a couple of muscular friends that could pull on the top and bottom of the roll simultaneously, while I ran up to the wall, threw myself against the exposed curved area, and flatten it by the sheer weight and velocity of my one hundred fifty pounds.

I transformed myself into a human battering ram, and kept up this insane effort for hours as the sky began to darken, my body screamed at me to quit, and the aluminum unrolled, yard by yard, covering my precious newsstand. People stopped to watch this unique display of grit and feeblemindedness, as rush hour brought the evening crowds home from downtown.

As each foot or so flattened, I pounded heavy nails into it to secure it, and kept moving forward. The hours crept by, the ringing of my hammer filled the night air as it hit the metal like a machine

gun—over and over and over.

The two guys stayed until ten p.m. and then left, but I stayed and wrenched the remaining six feet of the aluminum around the last angle.

The cops watched me, the lunatic carpenter, sympathetically, as the hours crept by, and realized I couldn't just leave things unfinished, with a jagged edge of thick scrap aluminum sticking out, ready to catch and really hurt some unsuspecting passerby.

A couple of the guys brought me a hamburger, fries and a thick chocolate milkshake, then stayed a bit to keep me company while I wolfed down the food. I hadn't eaten all day, and it was amazingly good.

Then they left and I resumed my hammering, by now much slower, trying to hit nails in the dark, street lights casting distorting shadows, hitting my hands, my thumbs, so tired, so numb, so close to the end.

By one a.m., the last metal curl was pounded out, nailed into place and the charred, fragile wooden newsstand was now like an invincible knight in one long continuous sheet of shining armor. **My Aluminum Fortress!**

I stepped back to admire my accomplishment, an amazing feat, I felt, using my body to vanquish the impossible foe. But I'd done it. It was finished, and I'd never do anything like that ever again.

My twenty-two year old body, very lean and hard from the endless work at the newsstands, was not sufficiently cushioned enough for what I'd made it do, and every inch of me ached. My hands were stiff from the hours of hammering. My knees were skinned every way a knee could be skinned. Every knuckle was bloody, and several fingernails were turning black where I'd hit them with my hammer, in the dark night.

Every joint: shoulders, elbows, wrists, hips—any part of me that moved was on fire from the abuse I'd put it through. I felt as if I were the rusted Tin Man, from the *Wizard of Oz*, with no oil in sight.

I leaned my back up against the newsstand to rest for a bit before going home, then slowly slid down the metal wall to the damp earth behind the newsstand, my bony ass hitting the ground with a thud. And I stayed there, too exhausted to move, all night.

But, at the age of twenty-two, your body is resilient. After a long, hot, steamy shower later that morning, giant plates of whatever food I could find in the refrigerator, and ten hours of sleep, I was pretty much recovered, only slightly sore here and there, and ready to go back to selling newspapers.

No one ever again torched the 53rd and Lake Park newsstand for the many years I owned it. Mission accomplished.

Amazingly, thirty years later, as of this writing in 2007, it is the only structure still remaining out of all the many different businesses I have operated since 1965. I must have done a really good job protecting my little wooden shack.

If anyone in Hyde Park gives a damn, I think they ought to make it a landmark.

Part V:
Loyalty, Corruption and the Chicago Machine

By 1975 I'd been running the newsstand for ten years.

As to size—always a topic of interest in America—my newsstand was sixteen by twelve feet at its peak as a wooden structure. Considering that the city newsstand permits were regulated by **(1)** the major Chicago daily newspapers, **(2)** City of Chicago ordinances, **(3)** local Chicago street inspectors, **(4)** the surrounding neighborhood residents, and **(5)** the local ward alderman—a very powerful person, as long as he was a Democrat, the only legitimate, recognized political party in the City of Chicago—some poor schlep standing outside on a God-forsaken corner, freezing his ass off trying to make two cents every time he sold a ten-cent newspaper, received more scrutiny from governing bodies than potential communists in Hollywood during the McCarthy witch hunt era.

Then there was the incident with the EPA guy.

That's the Environmental Protection Agency which, in a just and wise society, would be a very good organization to have around, to protect the citizenry from harmful poisoning of the air, and other bad things caused by giant corporations.

But I didn't live in that society.

One bitterly frozen Sunday morning in February 1970, I was working at the little open hut I'd set up across the street from the main newsstand—the one that had the heat. I had this idea that I could catch traffic going in both directions on busy mornings, thereby increasing my sales and taking some of the pressure off the larger besieged newsstand.

It had only been in operation a few Sundays and hadn't really caught on yet. But I was willing to give it a decent chance, even if it was only a newspaper stand.

God, I was freezing!

I went across the street to get a large, metal garbage can filled with bent wires from the newspaper bundles and the heavy paper the newspaper companies wrapped the bundles in, to protect them when they were flung from the back of the paper trucks, like cluster bombs. Bam! Bam! Bam!

The metal can was heavy and hard to drag, but I felt that if I burned the heavy paper in the can, it would also heat up the wires in the can as well, making the heat last longer and hopefully keep me alive until it was time to close the little satellite location, in about two hours.

I ignited the paper and soon it was really warm, and I felt much better. I also had a whole package of dark chocolate marshmallow cookies, with a kind of graham cracker base, to keep me fueled while I worked the corner.

I was doing okay—selling a few papers, keeping warm, eating my cookies—when a small car, with the distinctive EPA logo on the passenger side door, slid up to the curb. Inside the car, a small guy, with the face of a weasel, leaned over and opened the window nearest me and motioned to me to come closer.

I naturally assumed he wanted a newspaper.

Nope.

I could feel the nice heat pouring out of his little car, when the weasel spoke up in a tough-guy voice.

"Hey, kid! Don't you know it's illegal to have a fire in an open garbage can?"

I looked at this schmuck—so warm inside his little car—this little Hitler who had the nerve to bother a guy trying to keep warm on a freezing day with a little fire, as if he were saving the planet from some dangerous corporate polluter.

"I'm cold," I said, looking him straight in the eye, while chewing my cookie. I was thinking, "This asshole is too dumb to live." But you're not allowed to say that to an EPA guy, out loud.

He put his car in park and leaned over, closer to the window.

"I can't let you have a fire burning in that garbage can," he said to me, sounding a bit more menacing.

Desperate situations require desperate solutions.

I moved a little closer to him, still chewing my yummy marshmallow lunch, and I said to him, in a conspiratorial tone,

"Want a cookie?"

He looked at me like I was completely deranged, as if I could not comprehend his authority.

"Kid, are you nuts? Are you trying to bribe me?" The weasel was offended.

"How about two cookies?" I replied, raising the ante.

The look on his face changed. He looked *me* straight in the eye, reached up to my tantalizingly close bag, and deliberately grabbed two cookies. Then he slowly rolled up his window, still looking at me, slid back over to the driver's seat, and drove away.

I've read that all men have a price which, if paid, their integrity and responsibility can be compromised. The weasel's price was two marshmallow cookies. And best of all, now he knew it, too.

I never saw the creep again. After all, he'd been bought off, right?

The law said that a newsstand had to be open on the front, be made of steel, be no more than two by four feet in size, and only sell Chicago newspapers.

Well!

Only a total moron, bent on physical and economic suicide and absolutely without any political connections whatsoever, would ever consider that law anything more than a roundabout suggestion from, initially, a local politician to "make me an offer."

Running a successful newsstand in 1965 required **(1)** that you belong to a politically significant ethnic group in Cook County, i.e. the Irish (always listed as number one regardless of census figures); the Jews, who were only the Chosen people in the City of Chicago if the Irish chose them for something; the Italians, especially the Sicilians, a warm, wonderful people (Don't you agree?); or the Poles, and this was thirty-five years ago before there were a million Poles living under, over, north and south of Milwaukee Avenue; **(2)** that you correctly identify where the real center of power was in your ward; **(3)** that you try to pay that person as little as you possibly can, and still get an unwritten promise of protection, as long as you don't cause your sponsor public embarrassment of any kind; **(4)** that you never, ever forget you are there by the grace of that person, and that you are their loyal serf and ally if they should ever call on you for a favor; **(5)** that you never forget to pay not only the agreed upon, usually yearly donation to the "party" coffers, but also the periodic, mythical raffles, fund raisers and any other minor tax your protector levies on you; and finally, **(6)** you never, ever, even after they die or, God forbid, get voted out of office (about the same thing in Chicago) talk about any of this or, unless your mother dropped you on your head repeatedly as a young child, name names.

In fact, I'd really prefer to suggest that all of the previous comments are actually just...conjectures...of mine, and not necessarily based on any real, historical event or transaction.

After all, it's forty years ago, right? A guy can forget things, or should.

Further, loyal Democrat that I am, I can't remember any names of anyone I ever met, including my wife and children, even though all the now completely forgotten benefactors of mine are long dead.

I think.

I bet those of you reading these comments about my

extraordinarily restricted and controlled behavior as a news vendor, think these are an exaggeration and just an attempt at lame humor.

I wish.

It's all true.

I realize that this long, complicated list of political requirements seems simply ridiculous, since all we're talking about here is a lousy, wooden newspaper stand. But that was the political spider web I was caught in, at fifteen, when I chose self-employment over a job offer as a busboy at a local deli.

Were it not for my dad, who endured the Depression that began when he was seventeen, in 1929, I wouldn't have lasted a year on that corner.

He had spent forty-two months overseas as a radio operator in the jungles of New Guinea and other dangerous places, working for General MacArthur until he was mustered out, in 1945, at the age of thirty-three.

He made it his business to patiently explain bribery, corruption, and how to successfully work within Chicago's political power structure, to his young, completely naïve son, so that I might survive and succeed after I chose to work in such a vulnerable profession.

My dad wasn't concerned about ethics, or social reform, or damning the system that controlled me. His objective was to open my eyes to the realities of power, how to navigate within it, how to negotiate, even when there really was no fallback position and, most importantly—more important than making money—how to make friends.

Political friends.

How having an attitude of willing, nonjudgmental cooperation, of accepting my responsibility, however insignificant, to help keep the ruling Party in power, was the most important lesson I could learn. Because in a crunch, my dad advised me, if I was in trouble, if I stepped on the wrong person's toes, if I unknowingly caused some problem due to my youth and inexperience, even if I maybe broke some small law, innocently, the only people waiting to catch me as I fell were the people who felt I was one of "them." Part of a team, almost a tribe, regardless of race or religion, and considered it a matter of fierce solidarity and pride to save my ass.

While maybe in the beginning all that the guys on the lower rungs of the Party were interested in was my cooperation and cash, as time went by, they would ask me, whenever the opportunity arose, to do some little favor for the organization—run some errand, sell a ticket, check coats at a function, which I did in the Forth Ward in 1964 when asked by a very powerful alderman. They always knew who was willing to "play ball," help out, and make their jobs a little easier, and who wasn't.

These were very smart guys. Maybe they didn't go to Harvard. Maybe they were crude with their language, smoked huge stinking cigars, and hadn't a clue about who wrote the Bill of Rights and what they were.

But they sure as hell knew where the Mayor's office was, on the fifth floor of Chicago's City Hall, and how to keep their guy in it.

After a while, when it was clear where my loyalties lay, and that I could be trusted, completely trusted, if a problem arose, then the flow of concern magically reversed itself.

Suddenly, I was being tipped off about some sensitive situation and how to avoid being caught up in it, or maybe there was some local opportunity for me to benefit from, to expand my business, to make a really good buy. Well, I was their guy. Why shouldn't they help me? Wasn't that the essence of the Organization? You scratch my back, and I'll scratch yours?

That was the fundamental foundation of the Democratic Party's virtual lock on Chicago.

Opportunity.
Money.
Trust.
Loyalty.
Friendship.
Getting the vote out.
Knowing that you were never alone when trouble came calling.

This simple formula, once I grasped my father's patient tutoring, was enough to keep my little, later not-so-little newsstand in business for twenty years.

And frankly, as far as I'm concerned, newsstand or no newsstand, I'm still on the team. My dad's team. He coached me well.

There was great security in always knowing where I stood. That I was part of something that was bigger than myself. That there was a certain way to do things.

A system that worked.

I know about all the scandals, the guys in jail, the relentless incursions of reform, the snide comments about the insensitivity of the entrenched regime, and so on.

I don't give a damn.

I liked Chicago better when it was corrupt.

At least I knew where I stood.

LISTEN!! I WANT YOU SHOULD GO VISIT MY SON'S DELICATESSAN, GUBBELAH, (HE'S A NICE BOY, MY SON)... AND THEY HAVE SINAI HOT CORNED BEEF ON ROSEN'S RYE (IT'S KOSHER) THAT WILL TANTILIZE YOUR KISHKES...

A NAME TO REMEMBER:
"The DELI-DALI"
Hyde Park's Only Kosher Delicatessen + Bakery
IN The Village Centre, 51st and Lake Park

featuring

The Best Hot Dog In Town, With Everything On It — And Tasty Knishes, Kichke, and Salami; Fresh Smoked Fish Swum In Daily - Followed By Ivy League Schools of Lox - Have A Bagel Or Onion Roll With A Real Sour Schwartz Pickel — Top Off A Late Study Date With A Tongue Sandwich On Some Egg Chale — COME SEE MY Father's Moustache! Come Meet My Uncle Ziggy! — Go To Rexall Next Door For Heart Burn. But First... Come In And Nosh!!!

OPEN 7 DAYS A WEEK - 7:30 Am - 9:00 P.M.; SUN. UNTIL 5:30
PHONE: 643-0500

(Sunday, Come Pickup A New York Times At 8:30 Am At my

Part VI:
My Kosher Delicatessen Opens:
Hyde Park Learns to Love Lox between
Two Pages of Newsprint

As far as my restlessness after ten years of running the newsstand, I had already done about as much innovation as can be done with that kind of business, exposed to all kinds of weather, limited in size as it was.

My frustration and envy of friends and former classmates of mine who were leading more exciting lives only added to my strong desire to do something else.

But, what?

All that I knew how to do was related to what I'd done for the last decade, and couldn't really apply to any other enterprise unless I wanted to open a lemonade stand on another corner. I'd actually already done a kind of variation on that idea already.

In 1969, at nineteen, I opened a kosher delicatessen, of all things, in Chicago's Hyde Park with my father as day-to-day manager, while I provided the necessary capital for all the fixtures and initial expenses. And, of course, my labor.

At the time, it seemed like a really interesting new direction for me to go in, completely unrelated to standing on a corner, watching all the cars go by.

I picked a cute name, "Deli-Dali Delicatessen," asked my mother, an interior decorator, to select an appropriately appetizing color for the walls. She suggested mustard yellow. I laid the floor tile with my Uncle Ziggy who used to own a tile store—among other not so successful enterprises—and now lived with my dad. Ziggy would also work in the store with us, behind the counter.

I wrote the advertising and illustrated it as well, with humorous cartoons of Stella, the Pickle Queen; and also full page ads in the University of Chicago's Maroon Newspaper, while still running my newsstand seven days a week, fourteen hours a day.

My father and I relentlessly researched the local kosher food sources, compared prices, visited many successful Chicago delis, with me silently listening to all that was said as my Dad spoke with the Jewish managers and owners of the delis who were mostly around his age. Much Yiddish was used, and I understood more than I would have thought.

My father was a master hunter and gatherer of information and suppliers. I learned many valuable skills from observing him for twenty years:

Pick everybody's brain.
Learn at warp speed.
Be decisive.
Right or wrong, make a decision and keep moving forward.
You can always make corrections later as the situation become clearer to you.

Neither one of us had ever worked in a delicatessen before. But we didn't let little obstacles like that interfere with our ambitions. We had seven hundred square feet of space in the small shopping center behind the newsstand, right next to a giant Atlantic and Pacific grocery store.

The owner of the shopping center was a warm friendly man named Daniel Levin. Five years earlier, in 1965, he had allowed my friend and partner, Rick Munden, also fifteen years old, and I to set up our little four by four foot wooden shack on the edge of his property, then a mostly vacant lot. He now offered us the opportunity to open a bakery in a small un-rented space that was currently used as a storage room by the property managers.

He felt that my father and I were resourceful and energetic, called us **"The Katzman Boys,"** and thought that a bakery would be a romantic, nostalgic touch to make his brand new shopping center just a little more inviting.

My father quickly determined from his investigation of the existing Jewish bakeries—for this would, in fact, be a Jewish-flavored enterprise, and not some bland generic bread and cookie store—that we could not make enough money selling just donuts and coffee to the morning rush hour commuters to cover our expenses.

We would need a lunch hour and a takeout sandwich business to make a go of it. Deli trays, Lazy Susans, kosher hot dogs, coke—a wide ranging variety of foods to be successful in an area that was maybe only twenty-five per-cent Jewish. The rest of Hyde Park was about thirty per-cent black, thirty-five per-cent white non-Jewish, and perhaps ten per-cent Asian. An unknown per-cent of the highly independent and famously liberal and unusually socially active community was Unitarian, which was mostly Jewish, too, as far as I could tell. I guess you could be both, as long as you voted

Democratic.

Hyde Park also had socialists, communists, atheists and anarchist. For all I knew, Hyde Park had witches and Druids, too. It was a pretty cool place to be in the mid-Sixties. I think there was just something in the air that made it such an interesting and avant-garde place to live and work.

Actually, there was *definitely* something in the air. It was of an unusually good quality, quite inexpensive and available by the ounce, everywhere.

So we realized that designing a new business that aimed at only a small percentage of the local population wouldn't fly. We decided that we should offer the best quality of food possible, target the upper middle class and university crowd, and charge appropriately, hoping that the well traveled and sophisticated local population would appreciate having something reminiscent of the Old World Yiddish Lower East Side flavors of New York City.

Of course, I was born and raised on the South Side of Chicago, and had never been within nine hundred miles from New York. My dad was born in Newport, Kentucky, in 1912, then moved across the Ohio River to the mostly German Cincinnati, Ohio for two years, and then finally moved north with his parents Rose and Jacob to the old Jewish West Side of Chicago, until he became an adult.

But you can't let these little geographic details get in your way when a good opportunity comes up, so we figured we'd make it up as we went along. This is known in Yiddish as "chutzpah", or an unusually brazen kind of nerve.

So—we needed the whole delicatessen schmere to be successful: fresh chopped liver, with hard-boiled egg crumbled on the top; herring; corned beef, both lean and deliciously fatty; golden fresh smoked-fish, white fish; crunchy, creamy noodle kugel; gefilte fish in jellied broth; cream cheese; kasha; potato salads; lox, the queen of sliced salmon, both nova and regular; cheeses—American, sharp cheddar, blue, imported varieties; salamis of various ages and lengths—the long, smooth ones were the cheapest per pound, while the small, shriveled ones with the most intense flavors were the most expensive. Kind of the opposite of what you might expect, in another context.

We also would carry sweet coffee-cakes, sponge-cakes, scrumptious poppy-seed cakes, rugala with raisons and dates, cookies with chocolate sprinkles, Spanish olives with their pungent fragrance, peppery pastrami, freshly made crunchy cole-slaw, and fresh-pickled cow's tongue.

My favorite Jewish delicacy was roasted cow's tongue, when it was sliced so very thin, with tender white rice in a spicy, bubbling tomato sauce so aromatic I could eat a whole Pyrex dish of it—a European recipe that, regrettably, died with my mother. She once told me that if she ever gave me the recipe, that I would never call her again.

Now, I have neither.

We'd also crusty Jewish rye bread with caraway seeds, Russian rye, black bread, twisted egg-yellow challah loafs, a dozen kind of bagels, from sesame to onion, barrels of pickles: new, old and middle-aged, and more barrels of imported candies, monkey nuts and pistachio nuts.

And finally, huge hunks of marbled Turkish halvah, oozing oil, sitting like monoliths on our counter top on wax paper, waiting to be sliced into crumbling chunks for the true believers with cast iron stomachs.

We were two Jews who ate in delis all of our lives. My father since before 1920 in old world delis run by Lithuanian, Rumanian, Polish, and Byelorussian immigrants who brought their wonderfully delicious recipes across the ocean with them from the ancient shtetles of impoverished Eastern Europe, to the jam packed tenements of the West side of Chicago. I grew up with the aged remnants of those original deli operators, places like Ashkenaz' and Braverman's, since 1955, but I also ate in the more transitional delicatessens, now run by the grandchildren of the first wave over from Eastern Europe, with flavors more in tune with the tastes of a new generation of American Jews.

My father and I were Jews who loved our exotic foods, knew what "good" was, even if we had never run a deli before. But in 1969, we still felt that we could do anything, just anything that we wanted to do. I was nineteen years old, my father was fifty-seven years old, and we were a remarkable pair.

I knew early on that most older people wouldn't take me seriously. I was scruffy, with shaggy hair and very skinny. Actually, I look pretty much the same today, except for the shaggy hair and the skinny part. My usual clothes were baggy jeans and T-shirts, and I was full of nervous energy and ambition. I was game for anything.

But I looked about sixteen, and no one who didn't know me already would ever suspect that I was the self-employed, self-supporting owner of a prosperous, business employing a dozen people, from ten to eighty years of age, and that it was profitable enough to allow me to bankroll the delicatessen myself for $8,501,

6 wednesday, july 8, 1970 hyde park herald

Oy Vey! Katzman's opened a kosher deli

BY DANIEL POLLOCK

Robert Katzman is the type of fellow of whom friends and classmates might say in 10 or 20 years: "I remember him when he was just getting started, operating two newspaper stands on the corner of Lake Park and Hyde Park Blvd."

But it is a recollection which already can be made. Last month the 20-year old Hyde Parker added a delicatessen to his flourishing newspaper business. "The Deli-Dali," 1523 E. Hyde Park Blvd, is comfortably tucked between a pharmacy and a chain grocery store in the Village Center shopping plaza.

"I bet this is going to be one of the last of the schmaltzy delicatessens," he claims. And from the hand-lettered signs to the good luck autographed dollar bills on display, "The Deli-Dali" has the aura of a personable, un-slick business.

"The era of the small store is going," complains Katzman. "You go down the street and you just don't see the small store.

"You go into a chain store. You wait in line. You're shoved around."

The kosher delicatessen is dying out, according to Katzman, because there are comparatively fewer Jewish immigrants coming to America, who can prepare the food.

"You are running out of people who originated these things," he says. "This is the only kosher delicatessen on the south side that I know of."

He said there are kosher-style delicatessens on the south side, but adds that these stores serve food which is not "the real McCoy."

Katzman knows of what he speaks. In February, he observed the operations for five days at Sinai Kosher Sausage Corporation, 1000 W. Pershing.

The practical experience in meat cutting was only a small part of the preparations he undertook for the deli's June 11 opening.

He and his father, who is with Equitable Life Assurance, did much of the remodeling work on the store space, after Bob had designed the plans. Katzman talked with "other people in the business" concerning how much and of what to order. His mother picked out the paint color for the store ("I think it is masterium, or something like that").

From the beginning, the store had been something of a family project out of necessity. Because Bob has yet to reach age 21, his father must serve as his agent and technically owns both the newspaper and delicatessen enterprises.

"It is a real in-

"I bet this is going to be one of the last schmaltzy delicatessens," predicts Robert Katzman, 20, 1606 E. Hyde Park Blvd., owner of "The Deli-Dali" in the Village Center shopping plaza. Katzman, who also owns two news stands nearby, employs 11 workers in his businesses and hopes one day to go into real estate.

convenience," moans Katzman. "If my father doesn't want to do something, my hands are tied."

Initially, Katzman's father was "100 per cent against it (the delicatessen)" and Katzman realized he had some persuading to do.

"I knew that I had to convince someone who my father respects that it was a good location."

He managed to prove the merits of the proposed delicatessen to a north side baker, who in turn swung Katzman's father around.

Now, Katzman's father is convinced the deli was a wise business move and helps his son out in managing the store. Katzman has six employees working at "The Deli-Dali," and has another five who work at his two news stands.

"It is much better than working for people," Katzman says of his role as employer. "You never get rich getting checks!"

Katzman says he realizes that his enterprises are small but maintains that he would rather direct a less than large business than try to work up the ladder in a bigger firm.

"I would rather be the head of a rabbit than a tail of a lion," he reports. "When you are the head of a rabbit, you control where you go. Your eyes are in front of you."

Katzman started out early as a businessman. He collected pop bottles as a youngster, later sold fire crackers and protest buttons and served as a soda jerk at an ice-cream shop. He opened his first news stand as a sophomore in high school and soon was employing people to run the stand while he went to school.

At one time, he held down four jobs and attended school at the same time. He worked Monday mornings scooping ice-cream, operated the news stand on weekends, was an usher at a neighborhood theater at night and served as a page at the downtown public library every week day.

"I rarely did homework," he explains.

(Cont'd on p. 7

its total cost in 1969. In today's dollars, allowing for inflation, that's about $40,000.

I encountered age prejudice very early in my career—now called "ageism"—and I had to be resourceful to overcome the obstacles put in front of me by the older people who assumed that I was too young to know anything, or do anything significant. My father proved to be my secret weapon.

Irving and me on my second wedding day, February 19, 1978

Part VII:
My Dad, A Tough West-Side Jew
Class Begins: Chicago 101

We were already as close as two guys could be. He'd taken me in when I was thrown out of my home at the age of fourteen by my violent, raging mother, Anne. We lived together for five years, before I moved out at nineteen to my own studio apartment.

While some of that time together was stormy, and we had some aspects of a normal adolescent/parent relationship, mostly it seemed like we were two guys against the world, trying to make enough money to pay for our rent, light, phone and food bills, with just enough left over so that we could both chase girls.

After returning from World War II spent in the Pacific Theatre, and three and a half years in uniform, my father went from selling job to selling job. He'd been stationed in the Philippine Islands with the Signal Corps for eighteen months, working for General Douglas Macarthur as a radio operator and instructor, along with the rest of the United States Army in the Pacific. He island-hopped from New Caledonia to New Guinea to Corregidor, to finally participating in the horrific Leyte Gulf invasion to oust the Japanese occupiers from the Philippines, world history's largest, most intense navel engagement.

He spent six weeks in a post-atomic bombed Nagasaki, and was honorably discharged in September 1945 in San Francisco where, he told me, almost all his war souvenirs were stolen on his first night back in the United States since 1942.

His adventures were too many, his experiences too harrowing, including being repeatedly bombed, attacked by a kamikaze suicide plane, and once wounded by shrapnel, to try to shoehorn into this tale about his opening a kosher delicatessen with his teenaged son.

Like a lot of men I've read about—through my father I came to know fairly well—I learned that in many cases, for military veterans of major world-changing conflicts where either death or conquest were daily possibilities, that the rest of their lives were like pallid third acts of second-rate plays.

My father was strong, sharp, resourceful, and yes, a very patriotic American soldier. As the son of immigrant parents, he never questioned or debated the pros or cons of whether he really wanted to be in the American Army. He never looked skyward and cursed his fate.

His attitude, made clear to me over the years, was that as Jews, we were extremely lucky to finally find a safe haven in the United States, and it was a privilege for him to fight for his country. As the years went by, I found that I felt the same way. His values also became mine. I have been amazed, sometimes, by how seamlessly his liberal and socially progressive attitudes were transmitted, intact, to me.

He had an important job in the Signal Corps: sending messages by telegraph, from island to island, and division to division. Men's lives could be lost if he was too slow or slipshod in the sending of a strategic message, and he bore his responsibility for their speed and accuracy, heavily. He also had the responsibility to instruct and supervise this skill to the men under his command. He never again was involved in anything that mattered so much, after the war.

It may be, I've often thought, why he became so involved in my own struggles with school authorities, the police, and, for four long years, my battle with another company for the right to be their competitor in a market that they had long enjoyed as a monopoly. For most of my life, until my father was eighty-six, he chose to make himself my lieutenant, my defender and my never-tiring advocate. He once assaulted a man who spoke disparagingly about me in Chicago's Downtown Union Station. He picked the man up and threw him against a wall, holding him there with his fists clutching the man's shoulders until the other man apologized. He never told me about this incident. Other witnesses who were at the scene, who also knew me, told me about it later on.

Maybe it made him feel more alive, more purposeful than the endless series of what he felt were meaningless jobs that he held from 1945 until 1985. His last job with possibilities came in 1963, when he was fifty-one. He had passed an Illinois state test to become an insurance salesman for a giant company in downtown Chicago, and initially, things seemed to go well for him.

He came home jubilant, one day, in 1964, after working long hours for many weeks trying to get a small suburban town, to the west of Chicago, to let him sell them all the various kinds of insurance that their local government needed.

He used all his charm to ingratiate himself with the top politicians of that town, something he was a master at doing. Over many dinners, late night meetings, endlessly going back and forth between his insurance company and the small town's officials, he tried to hammer out all the intricate details of what could be, for us, a very big deal.

When he came home one night with the fabulous news that the town's mayor had approved his proposal, I couldn't believe it. It would mean the end of our week to week struggle to pay all our bills. We would actually have money in the bank!

This amazing, dramatic improvement in our existence called for a celebration: a winter trip to Miami (where else?) for the two of us on my winter break from my freshman year in high school. But this vacation was a bit misbegotten because of the significant difference in our ages at the time: I was fourteen, he was fifty-two, and we had really large and noisy disagreements about what a good time was. He wanted to relax in the sun on the sand, and I wanted to see everything, meet pretty girls, and check out all the pinball games that I could find. They were illegal in Chicago, at that time.

I did end up getting kissed, late on New Year's Eve, by a very pretty, very short Italian girl with long curly black hair. My father, probably got a lot further along in that department than I did, with the thousands of single, middle-aged women on the prowl down there.

We ate in fancy places, every night, and the money just flowed. I also remember taking a one-hour bus ride with two other newfound friends to visit the very tiny, very picturesque Cuban area on the outskirts of Miami. I believe that the ride to the Spanish speaking neighborhoods would be a bit shorter, now, forty years later.

Funny, sometimes, how things turn out in life. That trip to Florida, in 1964, was the last time my father and I ever went on a vacation together, even though we worked together, fairly consistently, over the next thirty years.

When we came back to Chicago, in January, 1965, my father got word that his insurance deal had, mysteriously, fallen through, and that some local guy, a relative of the mayor, would be selling them their civic insurance instead.

This news was devastating to my father, who thought he had finally broken through the impenetrable barrier of financial insecurity that had seemingly surrounded him all his life, and that he would finally achieve career success. This setback, the money spent on a trip that we never would have gone on normally, and other disappointments sent my father into a tailspin of frustration, depression, and fury. He never had an opportunity like that again with that giant insurance company, if in fact, it was ever going to happen at all, in the first place. He stuck it out, though, for five more years.

He hated every minute of it, despised his manager who received a piece of every thing he earned, and some days came home so angry, so red-faced that I feared he was on the verge of a heart attack. So when the Deli came along in 1969, he saw it as a way out of his terrible unhappiness, a last chance to be his own man and make a success of himself.

****

My father was the kind of guy everybody liked, right away. His strong, weathered, ruddy face was very appealing in a rough masculine way. He was no matinee idol, and earned the scars that he carried. He was such a solid guy, people felt safe just being around him. I know I did.

He was funny, liked to tell stories, and the words came so easily for him. He could charm you before you even knew his name. Women adored him.

Lots of women.

After he began helping me run my newsstand on Saturday nights in December, 1966, after I bought out my friend, I noticed that some new women that I didn't know would casually drop by the stand during the week. Women in their forties or fifties and good looking, too, quietly inquired about when my father might be "available" for them to visit. It was like a parade. Each woman that my father focused on for a while, and maybe made them laugh or blush, felt that they were his extra-special friend and they thought that a closer relationship might develop.

But that *never* happened.

Not then.

He had a big muscular frame, huge hands that he told me he'd gotten from endless hours and days of playing handball in his Jewish ghetto neighborhood on Chicago's ancient West Side, around 1925 or so. He also played baseball and had facial scars on his brow from when some jackass cracked him across the forehead with a bat, one day, "accidentally", as the guy claimed.

My father told me he got patched up and was playing again the next day. Tough guys, my father and his friends.

He bowled, played basketball into his fifties, and late in life even came to love golf. When I was in grade school, he taught me how to wrestle. He'd catch me in a scissor lock with his legs, trapping me, and then pretend to read his newspaper while I squealed and laughed.

He knew all the sports teams, all the statistics, the managers, the intrigues, the scandals—enough fuel for thousands of hours of conversation with cops, cabbies, mail carriers and just about any guy from any station of society that considered himself a man's man.

My father was the perfect person to represent me. His clothes looked great: sport jacket, casual, colorful shirts, black slacks—he looked handsome and capable. To my father, a necktie was essential to really being well dressed. We differed there.

He came of age during the Great Depression that began in October 1929, turned eighteen in 1930, and just as he was getting established after so many lean years of trying to find any kind of work, the Second World War snatched him up and he was gone for almost four years. By its end, in 1945, he was thirty-three, wondering where his life had gone, and once again became a salesman.

He did so *many* things: sold furniture, pool tables, beer coolers, mattresses and carpeting. He even owned a jewelry store for a number of years on the fifth floor of the Garland Building, in downtown Chicago, where he met many colorful characters, even, as he liked to say with a smile, some that *weren't* criminals. He introduced me to them, too.

With this varied, wide-ranging background, he looked like he could handle any situation and come out on top. He exuded confidence, seemed prosperous and had the air of a successful man. He also had, when necessary, a gritty, pugnacious street quality that suggested you would be wise not to mess with him.

His youth had been spent in Jewish gangs that frequently rumbled with the Irish and Polish gangs on the West Side of the city, and he knew from experience, as he explained to me patiently in his many stories, that if someone showed any fear in public, a guy could get in deep trouble.

While nobody his age used weapons in those days, 1926 to 1933—Tommy guns were for the mobsters—he told me he'd been in some dangerous situations with the always larger Catholic gangs, and he came to know what he was made of.

So I knew, and my father knew, too, that he looked the part of a confident businessman, worldly and experienced, and that I looked like a scruffy street urchin, who had just snatched an apple from the corner grocer.

But all of our lives working together, from 1965 through 1997, thirty-two years of struggles and successes, flush times and failures, I actually owned and managed every single enterprise, while he initially dealt with the landlords, the police and the corrupt politicians—and there were so many corrupt politicians.

We were two sides of one successful personality, and we maintained that duality all through my teens and early twenties, until finally I looked old enough to drive a car, or shave. Eventually, I developed the confidence to speak for myself, instead of through my father.

My father would come and go, job to job, than come back with me to work for a while, than go off somewhere else again. He was a restless man, and as soon as he had a few hundred dollars in his pocket, some other place looked better than the place he was in. He always had some deal cooking, some big plans to maybe make a bundle, but it was always cut and run—never stick it out and give some enterprise a chance to grow and really become something solid.

Part VIII:
Chicago 102: Payoffs
Learning to Survive in Corrupt Chicago

So I learned from him the coded language of how to pay off a cop for some minor infraction of the law. Or how much cash to offer a Chicago Streets and Sanitation Inspector to help him decide that my rambling wooden shack of a newsstand wasn't actually *eight* times as large as the city statutes permitted. Sometimes we communicated just with our eyes, very subtlety.

Or how to bribe the Health Inspector guy, truly the complete Emperor of his terrified domain. He shut down our Deli one incredibly busy school day afternoon, locking our front door from the inside after chasing out three dozen customers, and putting a **"CLOSED BY THE HEALTH DEPARTMENT"** sign on the glass facing out.

He evidently wanted to attract our attention as to who he was in our lives.

He did.

He held all the cards.

Five crisp twenties later, he smiled, pocketed our "compliance fee," shook our hands, and mentioned that he'd be back about this same time next year, so we could have his money ready. Then he removed his sign, and left our delicatessen.

One hundred bucks, in 1969 dollars, to stay open all year.

Twenty-seven cents a day.

What a *bargain!*

We never really had any serious trouble with the various City Inspectors. We knew the score. We followed the rules. All that these City Inspector guys wanted was respect, and a little cash, and why not?

If the Inspectors actually wrote up the seemingly endless number of violations that they could dream up, if they felt like it, it would cost us thousands of dollars to comply with all the city codes and we'd inevitably have to close the Deli. So the City guys priced themselves reasonably, for fast turnover, especially if you were a little guy.

Big, fancy-schmancy white tablecloth restaurants most likely paid the large bucks to make up for the financial shortfalls because of guys like me, to maintain the City Inspector's life style. To be sure, everybody paid. Nobody talked.

No one was fool enough to risk the possibly *horrible* consequences of squealing to the press, thereby not only endangering their own economic futures, or perhaps even worse, but upsetting the established status quo for everyone else, as well. God forbid a legitimate inspector should come in and everybody had to fix every damn code violation.

Mass bankruptcy!

So, I learned, with my father's patient instruction, how to survive and navigate in a neatly organized, dependably corrupt system where everyone had a price and all you had to do was pay it, and then everyone was happy.

Part IX:
Our Kosher Mouse:
Forty Years Later, I'm Still not Taking His Calls

There was one amusing, ongoing situation at the Deli that was never caught by the Health Department Inspectors, not that they cared: Mice.

We were next to an enormous A & P grocery store, and no matter how many traps we set, a never-ending flow of apparently Ashkenazi mice with a longing for crumbs of kosher corned beef and Jewish rye bread, kept coming over to sample our wares. I was never sure about their preference for mustard.

We tried fruitlessly to be mouse-free, but the athletic little suckers could squeeze through any tiny crack in our defenses if they caught an aromatic whiff of our Eastern European delicacies.

Hey, **Mousy**? How about a little chopped liver with some fresh onion slivers mixed in? M-m-m-m-m...so good!

But, ohhh, **Mousy**, you'll have heartburn so bad, I bet you'll lay your cute little dark-eyed head right down on our lethal mousetrap, and trigger that powerful spring all by yourself.

Bam!

Instant relief, and mouse-heaven, too.

My father had a humorously characteristic way of notifying me that a stray mouse was noisily rummaging through a box of kosher salt-free matzo. From our back storeroom he'd call out to me in a businesslike way, while I was waiting on customers behind the counter.

He'd come out and say, with a completely straight face, that "a **Mr. Meizell** was waiting to speak with me," presumably on the phone, in the back room. Meizell was pronounced: my-ZELL, with the accent on the second syllable, especially the way my father pronounced it, as if this mythical caller was some important Jewish guy impatiently waiting to place a large order of deli-trays, instead of actually being a furry little field mouse munching on our matzo, wishing he had a little chicken schmaltz to schmere on it.

One time I chased an elusive mouse all around the stockroom, finally trapping the little bastard with my broom on a wooden shelf about four feet off the ground, with no possible way for him to escape. Not right, not left, not up, not down. **Trapped!**

So the resourceful rodent must have figured to himself, "What the hell?" and leaped directly for my face! Oh, I was **mortified!** I really, really didn't like mice.

I swiftly ducked, my nineteen year-old reflexes serving me well, and that fearless flying mouse sailed right over my head, and made his escape.

After that wonderful experience, whenever my father would inform me that a *"Mr. Meizell"* was waiting for me on the phone in the back room, I'd tell my father to take a message and I'd call him back later.

It may be more than thirty years later, but I can still clearly see that Mighty Mouse leaping toward my face, hell-bent on doing something.

It *still* gives me the shivers.

Part X:
I Break with My Uncle Ziggy —
Defeated, I Leave the Deli

So the Deli prospered right away.

It was a rapid success and went a long way toward stabilizing my father's endlessly itchy feet. He was happy in his new situation, and basically ran the show, as I spent most of my time at the newsstand. A wide range of our friends and relatives worked in that Deli over the next six years, it always made money, and, for a good long while, kept my father's feet glued to Chicago. It always made money, all right, but not for me.

I, regrettably, made the amazing discovery that although I loved "deli food", and ate it frequently before opening my own delicatessen, what I really preferred was HOT deli food. Tender brisket of beef with boiled potatoes and homemade kishke in a natural gravy; roast tongue with rich beef-mushroom gravy; hot savory kreplach soup, with skinny noodles and a thin layer of shimmering chicken-schmaltz floating in golden circles on the top of the broth; and, of course, big, fat, juicy, dripping, fragrant corned-beef sandwiches cut so thin and piled so high on Jewish rye bread with caraway seeds that two hands weren't enough to hold the sandwich together.

And, oh my God, with golden brown, crunchy, onion-potato pancakes as big as your hand, hanging lazily over the side of the plate, with applesauce as it's faithful companion. Heaven on earth!

What I *never* liked, and rarely ate, except after funerals at the *shiva* house, was *cold* turkey, *cold* corned beef and *cold* roast beef. Icy cold fresh chopped liver was delicious, especially with crumbled hard-boiled egg on top and some bits of raw onion mixed in for a spicy contrast in flavors, but all that other stuff just repelled me. Somehow, during the whole preparatory stage of that exciting new venture: the investigation, fact gathering, supplier contacting, store decorating and the negotiating of the lease with the landlord, it never dawned on me that I really, *really* didn't like the food, or even the smell of it.

Even when I "apprenticed" at a local kosher meat packer in their small factory retail outlet, located in the industrial West Side of Chicago where the old stockyards used to be in Chicago's heyday as "Hog Butcher To The World", as Carl Sandburg called it, where I learned how to use the huge electric slicers to make thin sandwich meat, how to clean them, and, very important, not to look up when I was using the slicer—even then I somehow overlooked my complete lack of attraction to the product I was planning to sell.

Concerning that "don't-look-up" part, I noticed early on in my two week stint as a volunteer slicer, that most of the older deli men were missing one or more digits on one or the other hand. Sometimes, a whole finger. So I paid strict attention to what I was doing when I sliced salami or turkey, and soon graduated to retail slicer with all my parts intact. I even learned how to create complex and beautiful deli treys for parties.

But, back to my unhappy realization of the repellence of the food to me at the Deli-Dali. This situation grew worse and worse as I had to steadily put more hours in there and I was increasingly dreading the experience. I guess I never dreamed that such a good business that could generate so much cash could be so totally unsuited to me.

I was in a real quandary.

As if this miserable situation weren't enough grief for me, there were also some irresolvable problems with my Uncle Ziggy, who simply could not reconcile himself to working for his punk teenaged nephew. Our cooling relationship, formerly affectionate, at least from my perspective, made things even more complicated and unhappy for me.

Ziggy, formerly married to my mother's baby sister, Adele, and not actually a blood relative to me, had run a variety of restaurants and other enterprises over the prior two decades, but all of them eventually failed.

He was about twenty years older than I was, born in Germany, and had lived a romantic but volatile relationship with my Aunt Adele. I was very attracted to both of them as a child for their racy humor and youthful vitality. They were the most "American" of my older relatives, who were mostly immigrants from Eastern Europe.

They loved rock 'n roll music, and even won jitterbug dance contests together. Whenever I was around them, there was laughter, good food and excitement. Adele, only seventeen years older than I, has always been the closest, most loving person to me in my family.

But a relationship between two such high-strung people couldn't last forever, and eventually the friction between them, to my sorrow, split up their marriage.

My father and Ziggy, however, remained buddies for the rest of Ziggy's life, with me tagging along whenever I could, listening to their stories of their various adventures.

But as I grew older, and my newsstand business became more successful—especially at such a young age—and while Ziggy's fortunes ebbed, our relationship soured. He was bitter and somewhat jealous that his smart-mouthed punk nephew could make a go of a newspaper stand and even support himself, while he couldn't seem to find the magic formula to make his own enterprises prosper.

I was initially oblivious to his growing antagonism toward me. One, I still liked him a lot and saw him frequently since he was living with my father; and two, we'd never had any arguments about anything. I even worked for him a short while, when I was seventeen, as a cashier in his auction business, where one time I won the bid to choose whatever puppy I wanted out of a cardboard box, and chose my beloved beagle Mike, my pet for the next eight years.

As Ziggy's general attitude worsened, he continually spoke of how this current arrangement of working for me was only temporary, of course, and soon he'd leave—any day, in fact—to pursue his next surefire money-making scheme. He kept reminding us that he was bigger than this, working behind a counter in a deli.

His open distain for me broke my heart, as I really loved him, and I was just unable to comprehend his simmering anger even after I'd offered him a job at the Deli, since I considered him family, and he needed a job anyway. Aren't you supposed to look after your own family first when they need help? Why was our age difference such a big deal? How could I fix this depressing problem?

So, one day, in an effort to try to warm things up between Ziggy and me and ease the friction, I walked across the parking lot from the newsstand to the Deli when I knew he would be working behind the counter, to speak to him about our relationship. There were no customers there at that moment, so I told him how much I liked him, and that I was sorry about how unhappy he was.

His terse response to me was:

"I *never* liked you. I only *tolerated* you. You were always an annoying brat!"

It was so stinging, and so final, that I just nodded that I understood things more clearly now, and I walked out of the Deli without another word.

Newly knowledgeable of the impossibility of a cooperative, good spirited working and personal relationship, I resolved to settle the matter.

The next day, I went to the liquor store in the shopping center. The owner knew me and regularly sold me three cases of *Cutty Sark,* annually—even though he knew I was underage and that it was illegal to sell to me—which I would then give to all the newspaper truck drivers, each Christmas, in hopes that they would possibly quit stealing newspapers from my bundles for maybe just one day.

I purchased a small bottle of champagne. That evening, when the deli was empty of customers, and Ziggy was alone, I went in there with my little speech prepared, and spoke to him, briskly, like he was simply my employee.

"Ziggy," I began, "I know you have other plans to do bigger things than working at the Deli-Dali, and I really appreciate your assistance in helping my father and I get the place off the ground. I don't want you to feel any further obligation to stay here and keep from pursuing your other opportunities.

"So," and I then handed him the pretty little bottle of champagne, which completely surprised him, from the look on his face. "I want to wish you well, leave this small token of my best wishes for you, and to thank you for all your help. Good luck to you."

I shook his hand while he wordlessly stared at me, never responding, my words right then, fulfilling his absolute worst nightmare. I then quickly walked out, and went back to the newsstand. The next morning, my father came by the newsstand looking very concerned and said,

"Ziggy says you fired him."

I didn't say anything in response.

"Bob, he's beside himself, and has nowhere else to go. You've got to let him stay."

I nodded grimly at my dad, content that I had accomplished my goal of redefining Ziggy's status in my life, now that I understood his view of me.

And so, he stayed.

For the rest of his life.

****

Finally and inevitably, on December 30, 1969, six months after I opened the Deli-Dali, full of dreams of a new career and an eventual graduation from selling newspapers, I closed the newsstand at seven p.m., as usual, and walked over to the Deli as usual to work the evening shift. I put on my clean white apron to go to work behind the counter, then suddenly became violently, spontaneously nauseated, and vomited all over myself.

After a stunned moment, I took off my no longer clean white apron, walked out the door, and quit the damn delicatessen.

I gave half the Deli to my father, sold the other half to Ziggy, to be paid out over time and then, to many other people's surprise, went back to working full-time at my newspaper stand, completely defeated by the unforeseen.

But nauseated or not, I still tripled my investment in just six months, proving that a person can be a total schmuck about something and still not be *completely* stupid.

I didn't step back into the deli for a year, or any other delicatessen for at least five years. I was culturally dislocated for a long time, very frustrated that such an oddball situation could keep me from advancing my career. While my father and I may still have constituted **"The Katzman Boys,"** it was very clear to me that whatever cockiness I may have felt about life's challenges and opportunities just a short year before, at twenty, I was no longer "game" for just anything.

This defeat for me was quite sobering and also made me realize that the walls of my "paper prison" were much higher than I had ever thought. As a result, for the next few years I buried myself back in the newsstand, now undistracted by hot pastrami, eventually buying, as earlier noted, the only other two newsstands existing on Hyde Park's principal north-south artery: Lake Park Boulevard, at the 53rd and 55th Street corners. My newspaper sales just grew and grew.

I figured, "I guess this is all I can do so, damn it, I'll make the best of it."

My father kept his half of the deli for five years, until 1975, making more money than ever before in his nomadic life. He traveled extensively, and finally met and married the wrong woman, from another country, whom he found at a Jewish resort in the Catskill Mountains. That event quickly took care of his excess money problem for the next few years.

He eventually wanted out, but the lady resisted, until my father found out she had maybe, possibly entered this country under questionable circumstances. He threatened to have her deported, he told her, unless she divorced him, which she quickly did. That solved his wrong woman problem, permanently.

I guessed that while my father may have been a real prize as a date, maybe he was not so brilliant at choosing his life's companion. Using a sports metaphor, which he would have appreciated, in his case it was two strikes, and he was out, for good.

However, by then he was back in California and pretty much back where he started in 1969, except it was now 1975 and he was sixty-three instead of fifty-seven. But he was able to resume his carefree ways and date whomever caught his fancy, which suited him just fine, and that's pretty much how he stayed for the next twenty-five years of his long life.

Part XI:
Paying Dad's Debts with Kosher Pickles

The only proven good to come from the whole Deli-Dali experience was that my father agreed to turn over half his pay to me, each week, so that I could try to settle all his many debts.

My father had been perpetually in debt to a whole range of assorted creditors: Doctors, car repair people, credit card companies—all kinds of debts—and he was terrible about doing his own bookkeeping. The bills amounted to about $3,000, in 1969 dollars—about $13,500 in 2002 dollars, after inflation is factored in.

The past due notices were getting threatening, and this was years before legislation was passed that said the collection companies could no longer threaten to take your first born, which, actually wouldn't have been so horrendous in my case, as my older, perfect-in-every-way sister, Bonnie, was two years, six months and eight days older than I was, as she reminded me, daily, when we both lived in my mother's house. I suppose I'd have to give the collection company her address. Hmmm…

Anyway, revenge fantasies aside, since I was still living with him at the time, I couldn't help but notice the enormous mountain of paper as my father threw each new past due notice on top of all the other, unopened, notices, which were spilling over onto the floor. This cavalier, devil-may-care attitude, which made my father so popular with men *and* women, was not an effective way to keep the wolf, or in this case, probably the whole zoo, from our door.

So, again, despite our miss-matched public appearances, I was actually the much more organized one, and I seized the opportunity—the opening of the Deli—to exact a promise from my father, that if I could settle all his debts, then he would pay cash only, from that day on, for all goods, services and women that he wanted.

He promised. We shook hands on it which, in our personal code, was an unbreakable vow: A contract of character. He kept that promise for the rest of his life and died, debt free, thirty-one years later.

With that understanding between us resolved, I proceeded to call all his many creditors, after I sorted out all the bills from the humongous pile on his coffee table. I then threw out all the duplicate statements, thereby immediately reducing the bulk of the pile by *sixty percent* in volume anyway.

Then, as his nineteen year-old financial representative, I called each creditor and told their accounts receivable person that I wanted to make payment arrangements with them, in an effort to clear up my father's debts.

Well!

These credit guys, so used to hunting down debtors like a snarling vicious pack of baying hounds, would fall all over your feet, like convulsive puppies, ready to lick your toes, if someone actually took the initiative and called *THEM!*

They were so used to being the eternally frustrated pursuer of bad debts, that they were emotionally unprepared to deal with someone who wanted to voluntarily throw money at them. One by one, working my way through that impressive pile of obligations, I was able to persuade every single one of my father's creditors to, one: reduce his debt to a lesser amount, and two: give me a year to pay the remaining balance off.

I had already decided that I would pay all his debts no matter what, even if the deli failed as a business. But my dad didn't know that, and I wasn't going to tell him. As odd as it sounds, I felt it would give him a greater sense of accomplishment, and satisfaction, if he felt that it was him that was really paying down the debt, and just using his son as a convenient mediator.

Yeah, I know it's a very strange reversal of roles, but he did plenty for me that I was unable to do on my own, so who really gives a damn who does what? We were a family, a tiny, very tight family, and when the "hostiles" began circling our wagons, does it really matter who puts the bullets in the gun, and who shoots the gun, as long as it saves the day?

My father needed a break, I was in a position to help, and I would not fail him. I loved him, and saw all his realities, and foibles, even if the world outside of us did not. But the Deli-Dali did not fail. My father religiously supplied me with the funds to pay his creditors, and he was both relieved and proud that his son chose to get involved in his tangled finances. I know this because he told me so. We were not stingy about expressing our loving gratitude toward each other, when one of us could help the other.

God, I wish I had him now.

At the end of one year, all his debts had been paid, amicably, and my father said he felt as if an enormous weight had been lifted from his shoulders, and reaffirmed his pledge to pay cash only, from then on. Not every son gets the opportunity to really make a difference in his father's life. Contrary to feeling, as some might, that handling my father's debts was burden, I considered it a privilege to be able to help him.

At my sister Bonnie's wedding, in June 1975

Part XII:
Mish-Mosh: Corned Beef with Ketchup,
France, Mustard and Other Problems

Where was Saul Bellow in all of this?

You really want me to say he had an insatiable yen for our delicious hot corned beef sandwiches, and parked himself over in a corner of the deli, on Sunday mornings, munching on a tasty knish, while entertaining the customers with ironically humorous stories? Well, he didn't. At least, as far as I know.

After that last, gross, experience for me in the deli at the end of 1969, I stayed at that newsstand one hundred percent of the time, especially on Sundays when I was up to my ass in *Sunday New York Times* and their prickly purchasers. Who knows what Saul Bellow liked to eat? For all I know, maybe he had a passion for Ecuadorian tacos filled with kimchee from Korea.

Considering that Mr. Bellow's family most likely came from the same parts of Eastern Europe that my family came from, that is, Poland, Lithuania, and Byelorussia, where the vast majority of Jews immigrated from between 1880 and 1914, it is very likely he grew up on the Quebec equivalent of the West Side of Chicago, and ate the same wonderful food.

Not all Jews are as peculiar as I am and generally go with the cultural flow. I have learned from long experience and experiencing the gasping public distain of ancient deli countermen from Los Angeles' Jewish Fairfax area, to New York City's Lower East Side, specifically Katz's Delicatessen, to Wolfy's in Miami, Florida, that surely I am the only Jew that all of them have ever met that has to have his steaming, juicy corned beef sandwich on rye bread with caraway seeds, smothered in *ketchup*, to make it acceptable for me to eat.

I can't imagine eating a hot corned beef sandwich without it. Just what is this national obsession with mustard? Mustard tastes terrible! It must be an acquired taste, because I always hated it, and besides, I want to keep all the tastes I was born with, and I don't need to "acquire" any more.

Ketchup is good. Tomatoes, corn syrup, spices, water—all good things. It makes me feel all warm just thinking about ketchup— not s-a-l-s-a—that alien substance covering America like kudzu. Just ketchup. The perfect companion for crispy French fries and darkly charred kosher jumbo hot dogs. What a treat!

My mother, in one of her less pyrotechnic moments, introduced me to the scrumptious combination of ketchup and A-1 Sauce, in equal parts, as a tangy topping for broiled sirloin steak. The steak's juices mix up with the other two flavors and it's just *SO* satisfying. Later I added burnt onions to that recipe in the Romanian-Jewish manner. It made my mom's initially simple-but-wonderful condiment just a bit more complex—and crunchy.

But, mustard?

What is it?

Where is it from?

Probably...**France!**

One more reason to hate it.

The—"You will *never* be as cultured and ironic as we are, but even if you could be, we would still never accept you as equals, because we are...**Gauls!**...and beyond criticism, especially from lesser species, like (wrinkled nose) **"Americans",** who still owe us everything because we helped you trap the British at Yorktown in 1783"—country.

Well, thanks forever for Yorktown, Pierre, but maybe, during World War II, if a whole bunch of you were a little less enthusiastic in helping the Nazis with their Special Project one hundred sixty years *after* our Revolutionary War, there might still be another two hundred thousand French Jews around to consume your precious Dijon mustard.

But, let's just confine my contempt to the mustard. Even the color of mustard has unappetizing associations for me. It looks like putty. Not my favorite flavor. If I wanted putty, I'd go to a hardware store, where I've never noticed them selling hot corned beef sandwiches, except maybe in Israel because it's a real small country, the size of Connecticut and they have to use every inch of space.

Unlike, say, France, the size of Texas, which has endless room for cheese, and wine, and Film Noir, but, unfortunately, just not enough room for people like me.

Part XIII:
Saul Bellow Returns: My Gulliver's Bookstore Opens

Saul Bellow did reappear in my life, for the third time, in 1975, as a significant influence on my next attempt to change career courses and do something more meaningful with my life than giving some guy change for a dollar when he buys the *Final Market Edition* of *The Chicago Daily News*.

My original, and largest grossing newsstand burned down completely, for the second time, in Spring 1974, and my unusually nice landlord agreed that I could build a brick building to replace it. Kind of like the three little pigs. Maybe no one would huff and puff and torch my newspaper stand ever again.

Well, it's one thing to persuade an already sympathetic landlord that the brick structure that would replace the first little wooden four by four foot newsstand on his property, which had grown over the nine years I'd been there to sixteen by twelve feet, would be a real asset to his shiny new shopping center that didn't exist at all when I first opened it in August, 1965. My new "Palace of Print" would be expanded to twenty by forty feet.

But it's quite another thing to convince the Chicago Building Department, the Zoning Board, and the local neighborhood bluenoses who thought any person that sold *Playboy Magazine* was a tool of the devil, and so on.

I endured endless delays and contentious public hearings where, in one case, after silently enduring one truly venomous lady express her opinion that my international newsstand, that carried three thousand different magazines in *six* languages and employed *twelve* local children and adults, had absolutely no value whatsoever to the University community, and should not only **NOT** be expanded, but also should be shut down completely, I abandoned all self control, stood up and loudly told her to *just go to hell!*

Well, that plain speaking kind of response on my part did not endear me to all parties concerned, even if the despicable witch *was* threatening my livelihood. If this thing was ever going to happen, numerous hands would need to be greased, egos massaged, and tempers would need to be held. Unfortunately for me, at a volatile twenty-four years of age, I was definitely not the right man for the job.

It was not yet the time for me to comprehend that not only is it possible to not call "a spade, a spade," but sometimes you call a spade a " butterfly," or whatever is necessary to accomplish the objective at hand. I was just too blunt, had no patience for negotiation, and had about as much political finesse as barbed wire on a cow's hide.

As a result of my feisty involvement in the zoning process, endless delays in obtaining necessary approvals from the city, and other problems, no construction people could be hired, or even reserved for some unknown future date. By 1975, almost a year later, I assumed my little dream of fire-resistant durability would never happen, and I decided to try something else.

As it happened, I had long fantasized about running a bookstore, of one type or another. I felt it was a romantic and more genteel way to make a living than the rough and tumble, work in all kinds of weather existence that I currently enjoyed.

I loved to read, mostly non-fiction, history, biographies, science...was very good at organization and was located in one of the most literate communities in the United States, home of the sprawling, ever expanding University of Chicago.

How could I fail?

I could fail.

They say, or someone said, that if a person could really see into their future, they couldn't handle it: Deaths of friends, family, war, the Republicans winning another presidency, and other disasters. God, how I wish I could somehow have just managed a teensy, weensy little glimpse, and maybe my back wouldn't hurt so much today from all the endless, hopeless, pointless projects I've gotten myself into.

The fact that I had zero experience in running a bookstore did not deter me at all because, despite my grief, personally, with the Deli-Dali, it was still a big success five years later and I didn't know (or like) a pickle from a knish when I opened the place.

It seems to me today, nearly thirty years later, that my philosophy about business, and life in general was: When you don't know anything about something, then *anything* seems possible. Kind of like marriage, I suppose.

I have this "I'm older and wiser now" fantasy about myself, but fairly recently, I acquired a fourth child...um...sixteen years after the birth of what I assumed would be the last one; so, I guess, there's really no cure for my rampant optimism.

As of her fifth birthday, Sarah Hannah—a whole fascinating story just by herself, involving heartbreak, history and the supernatural, so, stay tuned—shows much more promise than any other truth-is-stranger-then-fiction adventure I've been involved with. So I guess it's all one really big crapshoot, no matter what I think I want.

Of course, I love the little green-eyed monster, so that puts her way ahead of the Deli-Dali.

Even though you already know the end of my story, it's still a pretty good tale. This, then, is what happened in the latest chapter of my twenty-year effort to escape my Hyde Park newsstand.

Spiderman™ visits Gulliver's Bookstore. I'm just to the right of him, in front of the store's window, in a white T-shirt.

Part XIV:
Where Do Books Go when a Bookstore Dies?

I found what seemed to be an appropriate location for my pipedream, a former long-time bookstore, in fact, at 53rd and Kimbark Streets, about four blocks north of the main commercial strip on 57th Street, where most of the university crowd shopped, had coffee, smoked dope, and otherwise rationalized their lives. It was on a side street, about one hundred feet south of the equally very busy 53rd Street, the main east-west artery of the overall neighborhood of Hyde Park.

I may as well have been in Siberia, as obscurely located as I was; but I was in a dream state, I think, and had no idea of what I was getting into, and so I plunged fearlessly ahead with my plans.

I chose a local realtor, randomly, who showed me the spot I eventually rented for two years, which was a garden apartment style store, half below street level of a university owned apartment building. When the lease was secured, and the place was cleaned up and ready to stock with shelves and books, I called my former high school journalism teacher, and friend, Wayne Brasler, and asked him to suggest a name for the store. I wanted something that sounded old and literary.

Wayne suggested Gulliver's Books, and I liked it right away.

It just sounded so right. So now, all I needed was an interesting inventory aimed to attract my target market, the university people, whom I should have known, after ten years at my somewhat erotically-stocked newsstand, liked sex, movies and rock n' roll like everybody else their age except, unlike everybody else their age, many of my graduate student customers ended up as physicists, surgeons, and law school professors. But I chose to ignore my long experience with the exact same customers I already had at my periodical newsstand that I was trying to attract to the bookstore, and advanced steadily ahead to my unknown destination.

After I ordered the sign, I contacted some book reps from major book companies, and other more obscure publishers and arranged appointments. I bought mostly remainders—previously published unsold books—that wholesaled for extremely low get-rid-of-them-at-any-price cost per book, based on the recommendations of the cultured, urbane book reps, who probably knew a *mark* when they saw one, and never missed an opportunity to unload whatever deadwood was weighing down their unsold book inventories.

These men were very tweedy, well spoken, with wry senses of humor. They wore earth-toned sweaters and expensive looking ties. They were very calm, self-assured and worldly men.

I was flattered by their warm, polite attention, college dropout that I was, and quite self-conscious about it, too, at twenty-five years old. They were such a difference from the bestial Neanderthals that drove the circulation trucks for the major Chicago daily newspapers, with their cursing, their unstoppable thieving of almost completely undetectable one or two newspapers from every bundle, and general distain for newspaper vendors.

Little did I know that I was most likely regarded as totally naive by the book reps, who must have quickly seen me in all my ignorance as a guy who apparently thought that all he had to do to open a successful bookstore, was "rent a space, add books, and stir."

As a result of their collective, gentle suggestions, I began to order books. Cases of books. Towers of books. Boy! I sure had a lot of books! Thousands and thousands of books, or so it seemed. Even if they *were* cheap remainders of unsold books about history, philosophy, literature, and religion—all things that I wished I knew more about—all those books still added up to many dollars.

My determined quest for gentility and legitimacy in what I did to make a living was soaking up many hard won dollars from my dusty, unglamorous but profitable newsstand business. But I wasn't done, yet. In an effort to add an even more up-to-the-minute literary sheen to my new enterprise, I wanted to carry new books as well.

I mentioned this to a friend who worked in the administration building at the University of Chicago, who suggested that I call up Saul Bellow, who was at that time a "Scholar-in-Residence", or "Author-in-Residence", or "Colorful-Celebrated-Jewish-Guy-Who-Wrote-Books-That-*Really*-Sold-in-Residence," or something like that.

I was able to get Mr. Bellow's extension number from the university's switchboard operator—no big secret, I guess—and I called him to ask for some advice about who he thought was a good quality publisher of new authors, or whatever he thought would help me attract the university community to my store.

He answered the telephone right away, and was very nice. He was always very nice. Just a warm, regular guy. I don't know...

Maybe if I sold hundreds of thousands of witty, intricately plotted books...I'd always be nice, too. **That**...could *still* happen. After all, I'm not even sixty...yet.

Mr. Bellow remembered me immediately, since I probably sold him a *New York Times* on the previous Sunday, at my newsstand. He listened patiently to all my many questions, and aspirations, and, after some thought—despite any misgivings he may have had about my latest enterprise, knowing as he did what my "real" profession was—he suggested a line of books that he thought were very erudite and widely varied in their list of international authors.

They were oversized trade paperbacks, very handsome and distinctive in their appearance. Kind of avant-garde and impressive looking, to me at least, when placed on someone's glass coffee table, next to a tiny cup of espresso. I struggled recently to remember the name of the publishing company and finally it came to me, but I'm not going to tell you. For all I know, they may still be in business.

But surely not in any way because of my contribution to their bottom line, except for my excessively large initial, and only, purchase. As soon as I saw the name Pablo Neruda on the cover of one of those handsome, shiny paperback books, I knew I was in trouble. It gradually, very gradually, began to dawn on me that I was way in over my head.

I was inexorably sliding, sliding, down to the terrible **"Land of Schmuckdom,"** a place no one ever wants to go to. Where all the hapless inhabitants have to wear blinking signs on their heads that say, in garish purple and orange letters: **SCHMUCK!**

It's a grim day when one realizes the extent of one's ignorance, and I was eventually awash in a newfound sense of self-awareness. Although Saul Bellow was kind, patient, avuncular and very willing to respond to my request for his suggestions as to what a good line of books might be to help make my bookstore more appealing, and who, on the one occasion I spoke to him about Gulliver's Bookstore, also wished me a sincere "Good luck" in my new enterprise, I never, ever sold a *single* copy of that particular line of books, in the two years Gulliver's existed.

Not one.

But man, they *sure* looked good on the shelves!

I made every effort to make that store a success, including adding a very diverse line of poetry periodicals from colleges all around the country. I also hired a local jazz group to play for a few hours in the store one weekend, in hopes of getting some positive publicity, and attracting a crowd that I thought would appreciate the off-beat atmosphere of the place. That particular event was a great success, in terms of having the bookstore filled from wall to wall with jazz aficionados. And the music was wonderful, too, but I don't remember selling any books that day.

Perhaps if I was selling old jazz records, or even biographies of jazz musicians, it might have worked to benefit the store. But, aside from the enthusiastic appreciation of that music-loving crowd, there were no measurable reverberations on our sales that following week, or thereafter.

Then, there was the problem of the...exploding toilets.

Actually worse than it sounds (you had to be there), that may have possibly been a factor in undermining my efforts to create a "really cool store." The geysers of sludge bursting out of the two toilets might have been a source of fascination to, say, plumbers, or maybe even vulcanologists who might have possibly been moved to compare the free flowing magma to Old Faithful, but then, they wouldn't have to stay and work there later, when the show was over.

Or help with the impossible job of trying to clean the floor up afterwards, either. Or reimburse me for the many books that had to be thrown out that were too close to the floor. It just wasn't the normal kind of stumbling block a young entrepreneur would have to overcome while trying to establish a new enterprise. I won't even attempt to wax poetic about the distinctive fragrance.

I think there are times when an author just doesn't need to provide vivid imagery, this being a classic example of one of those times.

Now, far be it for me to suggest that my landlord, the University of Chicago Real Estate Office, had any prior awareness of this amazing propensity of my plumbing to belch. For all I know, this may have been a **once-in-a-century event**, which means, of course, that *I* won the sewage lottery!

The U. of C. was and is a fine place, and not only because I was born there—at 57th Street and Cottage Grove, in 1950—but also because it is a center of learning known the world over for breakthroughs in physics, medicine, chemistry and economics. So many Nobel Prize recipients teach there, that the university probably won't offer tenure unless a professor has been awarded at least one.

But upon reflection, I think they're a little weak in sewage control technology.

For whatever reasons, one big one being that I was so far out of the traffic flow that my little, half below ground level bookstore was virtually invisible to the public, the store was a massive failure. I was determined to stick it out for the full two-year lease as a kind of penance, even though my kindly University landlord took pity on me and offered to release me from any further obligation after only one year. After all, I was **"Bob, Popular Hyde Park Paper Boy,"** off again on one of his zany misadventures!

But I refused their generous gesture, politely.

I obviously, to them, but not to me, not yet, hadn't a clue about what I was attempting to do, and I guess they wanted to let me off the hook, financially, before I did too much harm to myself. I was completely humiliated, quite frustrated by the store's failure and stubbornly insisted on paying rent for the last year of the lease, even though the store was already closed.

To me, at that time, it felt kind of like the cute, frisky little mutt puppy that wants to grow up to be a classy, purebred Russian Wolfhound. I once again reached too high and came crashing back down to earth, completely defeated. So once again, back to the newsstand, bleakly hopeless about my future prospects.

"Paper, Sir?"

Part XV:
About All Those Books...

When Gulliver's Books closed, I still had this vast inventory of unsold, un-returnable books sitting there, simmering, in the gloom of my customer-less store. All those thick paperbacks about history, philosophy, politics, religion, sewage—just kidding about that last one—sitting neatly on their unlit shelves, awaiting their fate. Well, I couldn't just *walk away* from all that effort. What a waste that would be!

So, after some reflection—something I could have used more of before I acquired all those many volumes in the first place—I decided to call my local synagogue, *B'nai Contribute More*, to see if they'd be interested in becoming the new owners of the books. I ended up speaking to a somewhat distracted older lady, Mollie, in charge of the temple's annual rummage sale, who said, "Sure, of course! We'd be happy to have you donate some books! Every little bit helps, young man."

"Some"...books.

H-m-m-m.

I'd carefully neglected to mention exactly how *many* books were involved. But, hey, God would understand, right?

I got some of my newsstand's teenaged crew together, and we spent a good long afternoon loading an unknown number of books, just cases and cases of books, wall to wall, front to back, top to bottom into my very large *Sunday New York Times* truck. One business burying the other, it seemed to me.

I then called that nice Mollie, and politely asked if I could stop by the temple and drop off my books. She told me to come right over. We could come in through a side door, and leave the boxes there. She would leave the door unlocked until she went home, so I'd better hurry up.

I asked her, kind of tentatively,

"Um...is it a pretty good-sized room?"

She simply had no concept of what was coming. Anyway, what could they do? Yell and scream that I left a few thousand more books than they were expecting? Free?

My eager young crew and I shot over there, as the sun was setting, and backed that big van into the temple's driveway until the rear of the truck was even with their side door. Then, in the gathering darkness, all five of us formed a chain—one in the truck loading boxes on the tail end, one unloading a box and handing it to the next one standing in the doorway, while one more kid began stacking boxes as high as they could go in the store room—while I ran around trying to push all the other boxes of toys, clothes, and miscellaneous rummage sale type junk out of the way, while we filled that room, completely, with the books.

Towers of Books!! RMK '08

We finished in about an hour of feverish activity, and then we all slipped away, into the night. I was not so much happy to leave the books at the temple, as I was really glad that I didn't have to leave them in that depressingly unfrequented store. Surprisingly, no one from the temple ever called me about the windfall of books I had left them. Not even to thank me.

I didn't care. Soon I forgot all about it as I resumed my change-for-a-dollar career on a full time basis, and Gulliver's gradually receded into the past, back there with the wreckage of other bright ideas I'd had, once upon a time.

Time passed.
Years.

I moved twice, got divorced, remarried, had more children, had some other equally successful adventures, and then, one day, in the mail, I received a fat white envelope from my old temple.

"Whatever could this be?" I thought. "I'm not even a member there, any more."

Curious, I ripped it open, and a very long folded-up adding machine tape fell out, with a short note from that nice older lady, Mollie, who had handled the temple's periodic rummage sales. How did she find me, anyway?

As I lay there on my bed, propped up with a pillow, late in the evening, I read Molly's note with disbelief, that somehow, she had kept a running total of the sales of that truckload of orphaned books that I'd left there, late that long ago evening, for a number of rummage sales that she'd run over the following years.

She thought that I would be pleased to know that *all* the books had been sold, and that the cumulative net cash total was over....**$10,000**....in revenues to the temple!

TEN THOUSAND DOLLARS!

I let the note fall from my hand, and flutter silently to the floor.

TEN THOUSAND DOLLARS!

Damn!

I sure could have used that sweet old lady to run *my* bookstore.

Well, I hope I've paid my dues for a place in heaven. Then again, I don't think Jews believe in that kind of stuff. Too bad for me, I guess.

Although I never saw, or spoke to Saul Bellow again, I guess he wasn't so wrong about Pablo Neruda, and that classy line of literary books, after all.

Part XVI:
Good-bye to Saul Bellow?
(Possibly) One Last Crossing of Our Paths

My final contact with Saul Bellow, although quite indirectly and kind of ambiguous, was on July 7, 1977, about one year after Gulliver's Bookstore closed.

No, I didn't write the day down like you would a friend's birthday and no, I don't keep a diary or have some superhuman ability to recall every event that ever happened to me, hour by hour.

No. I know that 7/7/77 date because that was the day the divorce from my former teen-aged high school sweetheart became final. But just before it was my turn to appear before the judge for final questioning and sealing the deal, a very short, very shapely woman was already standing before the judge, apparently there for the same thing. I never saw her face, but I deeply admired the part of her I was able to see.

Then my lawyer said we would be up next, right after Mrs. Bellow's case was finished.

Surprised, I responded,

"Saul Bellow's wife?"

He nodded. He seemed very sure it was her, although I never cross-examined him, or her, as to the accuracy of his comment.

I found this moment curiously ironic, that my path and Saul Bellow's kept crossing at such different periods of my life:

Delivering medicine to him on a bicycle while I was working at my first steady job at a drug store in Hyde Park, Illinois in 1964.

Selling him *Sunday New York Times* after I became self-employed a year later, at fifteen.

Soliciting his advice, ten years later when I made yet another attempt to escape my newsstand and move closer to his world of books.

And finally, if my attorney was correct about that attractive woman ahead of us in court…we were getting divorced, sequentially, in 1977.

All things considered, I would have preferred our final contact to have been a warm conversation over a hot corned beef sandwich, with ketchup, at the recently expanded Deli-Dali Delicatessen about the surprising success of Gulliver's Bookstore and the recent sale of

Bob's Newsstands, on that hot July afternoon.

But real life can't be ordered up like a pizza. Here, briefly, is a short snapshot of what really happened next in my persistent determination to succeed in the world of books:

Eleven years later, in 1988, I took over a failing foreign-language bookstore, transforming it into what eventually became a nationally known world-travel resource named **Grand Tour Bookstore**. I traveled to Frankfort, Germany every October, for a good number of years, to the world's oldest, largest book fair, and then traveled around Europe by train, visiting other bookstores in France, Sweden, Denmark and Norway. I nearly tripled the store's sales before the inevitable invasion of the giant bookstore chains forced me to sell the store back to its original owners.

In 2004, I incorporated my own publishing company, Fighting Words Publishing Company, published three autobiographical books under that imprint, and I've read stories from those books to forty different groups totaling about one thousand people.

Barnes and Nobel Bookstores now carry all my books in Illinois, and two more states, Michigan and Indiana. I've sold about twelve hundred books within two years, so far. My books are also on sale at The Museum of Jewish Heritage in Lower Manhattan, across the water from The Statue of Liberty. The Museum has reordered, twice.

I'm halfway done with my fourth book. I'm pretty sure I'll write a fifth one after that. How many people get to live out a fantasy like I'm living right now, as you read my stories? What happens next? Are you the type of person that reads the last page of a mystery first? Not this time.

It hasn't been written yet.

I'm still breathing, so, I guess...*you'll* just have to wait and see!

But I have to tell you, friend, this whole unexpected adventure is *so* cool...!

Saul Bellow
1915 - 2005

June 1961

2

An American Classic
The Kaage Newsstand
Since 1919, in Chicago

So one day in mid-October 2006, a couple of weeks before Halloween, this solid looking gray-haired guy whom I never met before comes into my back-issue magazine store, located in a quiet small town just north of booming Chicago. I don't know at that point that he was connected. You can't always tell just by the way a guy looks y'know.

Now, please, slow down...don't jump ahead of my story, friend. "Connected" can mean a lot of things, but in Chicago, usually it means someone is cozy with 'The Boys.' Not this time.

No, this fella asks if I have a life-size cardboard standup of the Bride of Frankenstein, because he wants to give it to a pal of his as a gag. Well, I was happy to sell it to him, whoever he was, because out of my original impossible-to-keep-track-of inventory of over 600 cardboard stand-ups in 56 different varieties, I was down to about 45 pieces, at that moment. I wanted to melt that vast cardboard iceberg of tied-up cash to pay my rent and other bills. Anyone who wanted a seasonal item like The Bride was very welcome because after October 31, it was back to the storage boxes for all the unsold Halloween Monsters for yet another long year.

The guy looks around, doesn't say too much, seemed surprised by my massive stock of over 100,000 magazines back to 1840, as I told every single living soul about who tripped across my threshold. Then, I usually say that there's only seven stores like mine left in the entire continental United States, in hopes the new visitor will get anxious and buy a magazine for the year his mother was born, before I suddenly close the shop up for good and maybe join my ancestors, like so many other antique magazine stores like mine have done, since the dawning of the deadly...**Internet**.

Like some unstoppable, unbreakable, steel fishing net trolling the bottom of the ocean for every living thing it can scoop up into its unquenchable gaping maw, the invisible Internet is killing untold thousands of small, personal, and frequently unique owner- operated businesses across our Planet.

When they first hear my voice, some of my new visitors pause for a moment, usually in surprise that anyone would actually speak to them, since shopping in giant malls can be a pretty anonymous affair, even with all those hordes of people pushing and shoving to get to where they want to go. Malls in Chicago have all the intimacy of Soldier Field, which is a vast open-to-the-sky football stadium parked on our famous lakefront, in case you're reading this story in some less civilized place than my fair city.

Some people gaze around in amazement at the floor to ceiling, wall-to-wall avalanche of periodicals arrayed before them, spanning the decades before the Spanish-American War of 1898. Sometimes their mouths hang open. Then, sooner or later, as surely as the dawn comes, my astonished visitor will ask:

"*Where* in the world did you get *all* these magazines?"

or

"Jesus, man...how long did it take you to collect all these things?"

Now, I do my best to be cordial and all that, but after forty-three years of assembling and organizing this Smithsonian Museum of Periodicals, all the possible variations I could possible have thought of to respond to those two questions, politely, have long ago been exhausted. But I try to hide my resignation upon hearing that inevitable query, and I now just respond,

"November 22, 1963, the day President Kennedy was shot and killed. I was thirteen at that time and I never stopped collecting."

Most people usually nod in response and then wander around my many long aisles to marvel at something most, especially the younger ones, have never seen, and too soon no one will ever see again. But I am always grateful for the business. I do what I can to be helpful to the newest amazed visitors as well as my regulars to make both happy, so they will return again, while they can.

Sometimes a couple of teens will pause at my standard response and I see them looking up into their memories to try and remember, vaguely, who John F. Kennedy was and then they just shrug. Those moments slam home the reality that I am definitely not thirteen any more. The major American newspapers don't even put the anniversary of his assassination of the front pages anymore. He's just some old guy now, floating through history and every day becoming a bit more forgotten.

Like Clara Bow, Valentino and Brigitte Bardot, all that blinding fame inevitably evaporates into dust.

****

Before most people leave my store, if I think there's a smidgen of a chance they'll be interested, I tell them that I'm a writer, that I've self-published three books so far (including this one), that I've sold over 1,200 books and that women buy 'em two-to-one over men, which I find gratifying, since all women know they're smarter than men, so I'm flattered by their approval of my books.

Some pause, flip through my books, turn them over to read the condensed version of my 56 years compressed into thirteen lines on the back cover and then when they see the second volume, provocatively entitled *Escaping and Embracing the Cops of Chicago* frequently ask me if I was a gang-banger as a kid. If it's an older man, perhaps remembering his own youthful narrow scrapes with law, he smiles at me and laughs to himself. Most women however, squint at the cover of my first book and try to see if the black and white photo of me, at thirty-one, is really me today, at fifty-six. They look up and down, first at the book, then up at me and eventually say,

"Is that really you?"

After I assure them that it is indeed a younger me, about half of the women buy a copy, mostly out of curiosity, I believe, because very few people actually get to meet the authors of the books they buy. Then, like one hundred per cent of the people who have already bought my books, they ask me to sign it. I am very, sincerely, happy to do that, all the 1,200 times I've been asked. Grateful people would care enough to ask.

After his self-guided tour of my store, the stocky, gray-haired, Bride of Frankenstein guy was again standing before me, listening to my brief description of my book's contents and he quickly stacked both books on my counter and paid the tab. I thanked him, slipped a bookmark with my phone number on it into both books, and then he left. I was pleased to have the sale, but after a few minutes, I was already talking to someone else, saying those things I dependably say.

After his self-guided tour of my store, the stocky, gray-haired, Bride of Frankenstein guy was again standing before me, listening to my brief description of my book's contents and he quickly stacked both books on my counter and paid the tab. I thanked him, slipped a bookmark with my phone number on it into both books, and then he left. I was pleased to have the sale, but after a few minutes, I was already talking to someone else, saying those things I dependably say.

Time went by, but not too much.

Though I was still unaware of it, a portal had just been opened, between my own past and someone else's present. Very soon, a person just like me...no — that's not correct...*exactly*...like me, or rather who I *used* to be, would be walking through it. Not a real visible door...more like...a rip in time. My dull routine was about to be disrupted.

Despite the passing of so many years, I would discover we still spoke the same language.

****

Though the decade when I owned a wooden newsstand is steadily becoming an ever smaller percentage of my life, less than 20% by now, for a long time it was the only identity I was sure of. Now that time is over thirty years ago.

In an effort to reconnect with that time and also with the Kaages, as I got to know them a little better, I looked through some stories I published in my first two books and came across this description of how newsvendors were viewed by the largely indifferent general public twenty years ago and how difficult it would be for me to find a job once all my newsstands had shut down, in 1985.

The people who didn't know me were not impressed by a resume that showed no college degree, and twenty years of running what to them, when you used the word "newsstand", was a small shack on a corner operated by people who were often very old, blind, disabled, sometimes drunk or mentally ill. Which was of course, true, but only for a very small number of the hundreds of Chicago newspaper stands.

I knew many vendors that were fine, smart, seemingly indestructible people, veterans of World Wars One or Two, who sent their kids through college with thousands upon thousands of nickels, dimes and quarters that shimmered through their callused hands.

But by 1985, that whole era was over. The very distinct culture of those rugged, independent people, newsvendors with their own special language and unique ways of keeping warm and dry in a world that rapidly passed them by, was dead, as were almost all the vendors I met as a teenager. But also dead was the newspaper companies' feudal hierarchal control of the newsstands by their often brutal, capricious and petty "Division Bosses," who had way too much power to determine how many papers you were allocated, based largely on how well you kissed their asses.

At the many companies where I applied for management positions, the young personnel managers that interviewed me one after another, and I was thirty-five by then, knew nothing of the nobleness of those tough men and women who ran those old newspaper stands, watched the streets, knew the cops, helped people who were lost, as I did many hundreds of times, and so often were considered an oasis of assistance under a lonely a beacon of light, usually a hissing Coleman lantern, on a dark street corner late at night, to a person in trouble.

Though those older newsvendors were heroes to me, who generously and patiently taught me everything I needed to know to make a go of my little wooden shack in 1965, those young personnel people, with no comprehension of my life at all, included me in that older generation and threw me on the scrap heap of urban history with all those other wonderful, long dead newspaper vendors.

No one, simply no one, would give me a chance, give me a job, and let me rebuild my life. I was like some ace Roman chariot maker, living past my time.

This second excerpt is from *The Taxman with a Soul*, about taxes I owed to the federal government, but was unable to pay when I was out of work between 1985 and 1987. The IRS hounded me relentlessly and made my already miserable life a living hell:

> *Everyone* in Hyde Park knew me. I sold newspapers there for a dime, later for a quarter, to anybody, everybody, seven days a week, for decades. I was that guy on the corner who stood outside your window, in the rain, water dripping off my face as I tried to keep your newspaper dry and give you the right change.
>
> I was the guy in the thick boots, heavy winter coat, in earmuffs and a scarf wearing gloves with half of the fingers cut off so I could still make the correct change in the sleet and the snow, a fog of my breath surrounding my face as I stood there, twelve hours a day, freezing, next to a useless kerosene heater, winter after winter after winter, waiting to sell you a newspaper, when you wanted one.
>
> I was **Bob**, damn it, that guy on the corner, not some wise-ass rich white guy trying to screw the government. I was **Bob**, and now I had nothing. Not even a damn newsstand."

****

One afternoon in early November, this guy ambles into my store, kind of tentatively, looking around for a sign of life among the ocean of periodicals climbing up my walls. Then his gaze lands on me and he walks over to where my register is, in a spot that lets me pretty much keep an eye on the whole store, especially the adult section.

The guy's about five feet-ten inches, seems near my weight— about one hundred eighty—has a salt and pepper beard on a boyish face, with shy eyes peering out of standard-issue glasses. No frills about him. No glamour. He is who he is.

He stuck out his hand, introduced himself to me and told me his name is Mike Kaage. His hand was hard, calloused and strong. A hand eerily identical to mine.

He said he and his family run the oldest remaining newsstand in Chicago at 6700 Northwest Highway, an angled street that is very difficult to pinpoint, when someone wants to give you directions to find someplace located there. The Kaage Newsstand was officially opened in 1919 when Chicago first issued permits, but most likely some kid was out there hawking newspapers for a penny at the turn of the century. Newspaper people know a good traffic corner when they see one.

Kaage's grandfather bought the corner permit rights to be there in 1943 for $100 cash and there's been a Kaage out there—usually two—for four generations. Most of them are named Irvin: Irvin Louis, Sr., Irvin, Jr., Irvin III and now Irvin IV. Plus Mike, of course, second son of Irvin, Jr., younger brother of III, uncle of IV, and most importantly to my story, a good friend of Raymond Falborski. Ray, whose regular job is a shipping dock worker, is the man who came to my store to buy the cardboard "Bride" and then rigged it up with a sign that said:

Take A Foto With Your Ex-Wife—$5.00

Ray   **Mike**

Ray evidently read my autobiographical first book entitled: *Bob's Newsstand 1965--1985,* and apparently ran over and gave it to his pal, Mike, telling him, in effect, that,

May 1950

".....here's a book about someone who really understands our lives...a guy who really gets it. You should read it. He's one of us."

Mike said he was in my store, to buy some more copies of my books to give to friends. As a former newsvendor myself, I immediately offered him a discount, but to my surprise he said,

"No, Bob. You gotta make a living too."

Nobody says that

I was wary. I wanted to sell my books and get better known as a writer, but I couldn't figure out his angle. No one is *that* nice. But Mike kept talking, not really shy at all, and we compared notes about our lives, our similar ages, that both of us worked at our newsstands with our father, the difficult misery that winter cold and snow cursed us with and that, yeah, I used to have pretty girls come hang out at my newsstand, too, thirty years ago...just like his place now.

While I was talking to him, I was watching him, too. Even if long ago I ran a chain of newsstands — there are so few left today, not only in Chicago, but across the United States — my being with him made me almost feel like an anthropologist discovering a disappearing tribe of indigenous natives, still practicing mostly long abandoned skills now considered superfluous by the general population.

But everything he said was so familiar to me, still so fresh...all his problems, his pleasures. Here standing before me was one of the few people left who could truly understand *me*. People talk about *"mirror images"* but, man, let me tell you...it is one weird experience to meet...yourself...in the middle of a random day.

****

But everything he said was so familiar to me, still so fresh...all his problems, his pleasures. Here standing before me was one of the few people left who could truly understand *me*. People talk about *"mirror images"* but, man, let me tell you...it is one weird experience to meet...yourself...in the middle of a random day.

Except Mike had never heard of what I...once upon a time...was very used to hearing described as:

"The *Famous* Bob's Newsstands"

Well, so much for the transitory nature of fame. But I had also never heard of him and his much older operation, even though I believed I was really familiar with all the significant newsstands left in the City. Mike's business was forty-six years old before I opened my first four by four foot wooden shack in Hyde Park, in 1965, and his newsstand has remained open and thriving twenty-two years after I had to shut mine down, in 1985.

Truly, he---*not* me---was history.

Mike and I shook hands, I thanked him for buying the additional books and as he smiled and was leaving, I wished him well and told him I hoped the winter wasn't too hard on him. I knew, that *he* knew, *exactly* what I meant. We spoke the same language, which, ironically usually involved stoicism and very few spoken words at all.

I knew so well he would soon be struggling to get through another damn frozen, sub-zero day with Chicago's icy daggers of fierce wind cutting right through him.

After the door closed I thought about what a gentle man he was, but I also figured, well, that was that, and most likely I would not be seeing him again.

Then the parade of other people started coming, sent by Mike, to buy my books...all friendly hard-working types, the kind of men who make friends and shoot the breeze with newsvendors. Upbeat, humorous...and arthritic.

Who *was* this guy?
Why was he helping me?
Nobody's *that* nice!

I decided to go see him and meet his dad, Irvin, Jr. A longtime numbers geek, I quickly discovered that Mike's ancient newsstand was 4.3 miles away from mine. So near to me...and yet, still so far away.

What I came to understand, after I visited his very modest, city regulation steel newsstand, met his dad and then watched them interact with their many customers was: Damn! They really are that nice! Not just to me, to everyone. Their customers, a river of them, were smiling and openly affectionate in their greetings to the father and son Kaages as they approached the corner stand to buy a paper, or just to say "Hi." So, I thought, everybody knows them.

Then, a very different thought: Mike buys my books and gives them away because, really, *nobody* knows them. He found someone, like him, who long ago left his tribe and now writes just like the

Training starts early

There's nothing like getting an early start in the family business. Three generations of Irv Kaages got together recently at the Kaage's Corner newsstand, Oliphant and Northwest Hwy., where Grandpa Irv II was on duty. Both Irv III and his brother Mike grew up working at the family newsstands and although young Irvie, 1½, wasn't ready to start folding papers or selling Reviews, he clearly enjoyed the visit.

November 1979

people in the newspapers they sell every day. Blending in with all the people like he was really one of them. Someone who could not only tell his story, but also all the newsvendors' stories. To him, maybe I was the guy who could leave a record of who they are, and what they've been through over the past sixty-four years, standing there by the curb waiting to sell newspapers to their neighborhood, every single day of the year.

It was a very sobering thought. These guys didn't have to be Western Union for me to get the message, man. Being with them, at their newsstand, felt so comfortable, so familiar, and so... well...compelling...to me. It would be difficult for anyone not part of that life to really understand why anyone could possibly miss doing something so physically demanding. Maybe I could do something about that, like being a sort of translator who had lived in both worlds.

So right there, I decided: Their time is *now.* I'll be their messenger. I'll leave their record, their footprint in the sand before the last few of them...no *us*, damn it...are washed away. And forgotten in a world of beeps, blips, iPods and whatever the hell people can think of next. Why? Because they god-damn deserve it. Pay some attention

December 2006

The Kaage Women - April 2006

Mike's sister, Patricia (7/7/54)
Mike's daughter, Kristen (3/12/85)
Mike's mom, Muriel Planz Kaage (5/18/29)

Newspaper customers often stop a minute extra to chat with the Kaages. The big special news in recent days at the Kaage Korner has been the wedding Friday, Nov. 23, of young Irv Kaage Jr., and his bride, Laurel Thoren, whom he's gone with since their Taft student days.

November 1973

to the anonymous men and women, who sell the news to the world, one paper at a time.

What difference do the Kaages make, some indifferent person may think, if he reads these words? What does it matter if I buy my newspaper from a coin box on a corner, or read it on my Blackberry whatever? Who needs the newsvendors? Why are they so special?

Well……..

Maybe once you were lost, late at night, everyplace is closed...except the kerosene lantern glowing on the corner tells you that someone is there, someone to help you find your way. Even though both of you are strangers to each other, somehow you just know he won't brush you off.

Maybe you're in a bad accident with your car, all smashed up and hurt, and the guy on that corner you never even met runs over to see how you are, calls the cops, calls your parents, calms you down and suddenly he matters to all those people very much.

Maybe you're a young cop, lonely, new to the beat and don't know a soul and one quiet night you wander over to that old guy on the corner who fills you in on all the secrets of the neighborhood, who to watch out for, where the bad guys hang out...nuts and bolts stuff a new guy needs to fit in, do the job and not screw up...well, to a young cop, that old man is Street Level Graduate School.

Maybe you're a punk, all smart mouth and no brains, too wise to get a job, to dumb to see you're going nowhere...and you slide up to that newsstand on the corner thinking you can snatch a Playboy, real fast, and race away down the alley...and that dopey old guy standing there would never know it, when suddenly....**WHAM!!**....faster than you could possibly imagine, that old guy's lighting hands, the ones that lifted thousands of too heavy Sunday supplement bundles, cut uncountable steel wires with a small dull wire cutter and are now gripping your shaking hands like a vice, the old guy with the *very* hard muscles under all his shabby protective clothing who now has your complete and undivided attention. He could call the cops...he knows *all* the cops and they'd give you a really hard time because he's their pal and they look out for him, just as he does for them...he could get you into some real shit you never dreamed of...but then, to your utter astonishment, he doesn't do any of that.

Father and Son: Irvin and Mike...(both photos: Dec. 2006)

Mike, Irvin and best pal, Ray

He demands to know what the hell you're doing, who do you think you are, what kind of asshole steals magazines from a newsstand, would you like those hard as stone hands of his to slap you across the mouth a few times, why don't you shape up, go to school, get a job, stop being a jerk, because the road you're on is gonna get you hurt real bad by the *next* guy you try to rip off...and then, muttering and cursing, he lets you go and turns to sell a paper to another car, forgetting you, sure you got the message, hoping you're not too dumb to recognize a real break when you're getting one.

Maybe that mean old guy tilted your life a few degrees in a better direction. Maybe your close call with a guy you stupidly underestimated (like so *many* people foolishly underestimate newspaper vendors) made you see you had a choice. Maybe you grow up a little straighter than you might have, because someone with a very rough daily existence cut you some slack because he *knew*, in his gut...that a little mercy can make a big difference in a young guy's life...if there's still any good left in the punk at all.

****

That's who the *Kaages* are.

That's who *I* am.

That's who *all* the few of us that still exist in this country are.

And *don't* you forget it.

A couple a Polish guys standing on a corner, watchin'
all the girls go by...Author and Irvin, veteran
newsvendors.

Kaage Newsstand, originally established in 1919, and
still in business in 2007, 88 years later.

Bob Katzman, founder of Bob's Newsstands
1965 to 1985
Gone, forgotten, just another tumbleweed of Chicago
history

"Don't cry for me, corner newsboys... ... ..."

Stacked below are twenty-seven bundles of Kaage Newsstand Sunday supplements, approximately 540 inserts, ammunition to load into hundreds of Sunday newspapers for their many loyal customers.

For the record:

Bob's Newsstand in Hyde Park, at its peak in the Seventies, sold 5,000 Sunday Chicago Tribunes, Chicago Sun-Times, and New York Times, every weekend.

Or the equivalent of 250 of the above bundles, an astounding amount labor that required ten boys to assemble complete newspapers, beginning in the middle of the night.

It was a staggering responsibility to organize all those boys and all those bundles. When I wax nostalgic about days gone by, no matter how much I try, there is no way to romanticize 5,000 fucking newspapers.

This page
intentionally
left blank

*Finally, about a month before my graduation in June 1968, my newsstand had grown successful enough that I was able to put together the thousand bucks I owed to the Whiny Voice. But before I did that, I decided to make a kind of **statement,** to reflect my four years of frustration and antagonism with my endless shortage of cash to pay them...and everyone else.*

The story that follows is about what I did to fully express my "inner child," after four years of receiving irritating phone calls trying to get me to pay up my delinquent tuition.

Oh, I paid up, alright.

*My **way.***

3

The Thousand Dollar Bill

After I left my South Side Chicago home, suddenly, the night of June 8, 1964, and moved in with my father in Hyde Park, I lost all my familiar ways to make pocket money. I'd never received any allowance, so if I wanted something, I had to figure out a way to earn the money to pay for it.

Beginning at the age of five, in 1955, I dragged my big red American Flyer wagon through the vacant prairies near the vocational school, CVS, on 87th Street, looking for discarded pop bottles thrown there by the teenagers. I then redeemed whatever Coke, Pepsi or 7-Up bottles I could find that were unbroken, for cash at the corner drug store near my home, which in turn I spent on squirt guns and chocolate. I always found some way to make a dollar.

By sixth grade, in 1961, I was selling coin collecting folders from the Whitman publishing company in Wisconsin to my classmates. I bought them wholesale from my girlfriend's father, Carl, a Russian-Jewish immigrant who worked for Whitman's and who was amused by my industriousness. I got along much better with the father than his cute, button-nosed daughter. Girls were a lot harder to figure out. However her mom, Eleanor, and I got along just fine, and she fed me handfuls of pastel-colored miniature marshmallows whenever I visited her daughter. Which was often.

My classmate customers began filling up the thin blue folders with Lincoln pennies, Buffalo nickels, the occasional 1901 Indian cent that still could be found in pocket change back then, silver Roosevelt or Liberty dimes, Walking Liberty or Washington quarters, and Franklin Half-Dollars.

I also sold them hardcover Blue Books, that told them what the coin dealers paid for collectable coins, and Red Books, that told them how much those same dealers would then charge for those coins. Also, the two books gave total yearly mintage figures for every single coin listed in their tables. That explained why some of the coins from the same year, but minted by different U. S. Mints in Denver, San Francisco, New Orleans and Philadelphia in smaller quantities, were sometimes much more valuable than others.

Those indispensable and widely respected books also attempted to educate all young coin collectors about the concept of grading coins according to their wear and condition, and importantly, how condition affected value.

By then I was reading Coin World Newspaper every week, out of Iola, Wisconsin, and a couple of monthly coin magazines. I acquired an encyclopedic awareness of which United States coins were rare, which were just pocket money, and all the fine gradations between conditions. My intense involvement with numismatics was not typical of an eleven year-old kid, but I saw very clearly that comprehensive knowledge was essential in the buying and selling of coins, which was the next logical step in my playground enterprise.

My classmates' initial fascination with coin collecting waned, as their interest in figures switched from pennies to girls. They frequently sold their collections back to me for much less than their Red Book value, so that they'd have enough money to buy their new girlfriends ice cream. So, my having ready money was essential if I was to be able to pay what these ardent young lovers wanted on-the-spot for their collections. My own coin collection however, bloomed.

While all this enterprise suddenly stopped after I was ejected from my house when I was fourteen, I held on to that very large coin collection for twenty more years, until 1985, eventually selling it to start the back-issue magazine store that I operate today, in 2006, another twenty years later.

All those copper half-pennies, pennies, nickels, silver three-cent pieces, dimes, quarters, half-dollars and huge silver dollars magically transformed into what eventually became an amazing store full of one hundred thousand magazines dating back to 1840, one of seven such stores left in America, by 2006.

Curiously, also in grade school, I managed to buy 1963 Playboy Magazines from cooperative druggists who didn't give a damn that it wasn't legal to sell them to a thirteen year-old kid. I then carefully cut the pictures of the naked women out of the magazines and sold them, one by one, to my horny classmates, who were not as adept at obtaining those same thrilling magazines.

I imagine they traded them like baseball cards, including their best adolescent estimations of the lovely models' vital statistics. Since my customers interests had switched from hard coins to soft girls, I had to adjust to new marketing opportunities. One could say, I kept...abreast...of demand.

Forty years later, I now have ten thousand American Playboys. Also, over one thousand different foreign editions from twenty countries: Hungary to South Africa and Russia to Brazil, covering the years 1953 to 2005.

Playboy Magazine's customer service department recommends me as a reliable source for back issues that they don't have. As a final irony to my lifelong connection to *Playboy*, the magazine's editorial office in New York City called me in January 2006 to interview me. I asked the interviewer why and he told me that my store was the last place in America that a person could just walk into, ask for any of over six hundred different issues going back to 1955 and be able to purchase them on the spot. The man then told me that my interview would appear in the back pages of the August 2006 issue. It did.

I knew this would happen. Now the human and the magazine have finally merged. I've become "Playman!" Today, however, I no longer cut up the magazines.

How many people continue to do a variation of something they did when they were thirteen, forty-three years later, at fifty-six years old, unless they were someone like Vladimir Horowitz?

The point of detailing all this history, is to say that I was always enterprising and tried to pay my own way, from kindergarten on up. But when I started over in a new high school, an expensive private school in Hyde park, part of the University of Chicago, where I didn't know anyone, had no connections and no income whatsoever, I ran into a brick wall trying to get a job in that strange new neighborhood.

I soon learned that a skinny, fourteen year-old boy, with braces and unfashionable clothes, was *not* a real hot commodity in very sophisticated Hyde Park. But I persisted, and reported my lack of success, daily, to my sympathetic father, who was having his own problems trying to make a buck.

After being turned away by the corner drugstore, down the block from our apartment, a couple of times, as either a bike-riding delivery boy or as a bus boy hauling big tubs of dirty dishes for their lunch counter, I became very discouraged.

My father must have noticed this.

One day, when I came home from my freshman year at that expensive high school, my father told me to go run down to the corner because that very same drugstore called looking for me, saying that they *now* had a job opening for a delivery boy.

But...I smelled a rat.

Saying nothing about my suspicions to my dad, I obediently walked out of the apartment, closed the door and walked noisily toward the elevator. Then, I tip-toed back and listened with my ear against the old wooden door to our one bedroom apartment .

I could hear my dad dialing the phone, waiting and then assuring the druggist that I was on my way to see him that very minute and that he, my father, would pay my weekly salary just as the druggist and my father had previously agreed.

I quietly walked away from the door, ran down the five flights of stairs to the first floor, accepted the "job" at the drugstore and said nothing about it to my father for the next seven days.

When I received my first paycheck, I asked the druggist to please cash the check, which he did. Then I went home and waited for my father. When he finally arrived at our apartment a couple of hours later, tired, frustrated and equally discouraged about his own prospects, I waited until after we had our dinner.

Then, I walked over to where he was sitting, sipping from a cup of steaming, scalding hot tea, just like Jacob, his immigrant Russian-Jewish father used to do.

I took all the money that I'd received from my paycheck that day out of my pocket, laid it on the table in front of him and said,

"Dad, if I can't make it on my own, I don't want a pretend job, paid for by you."

He was visibly startled by my words and my apparent discovery of his ruse to raise my spirits. But he smiled at me with a new appreciation that my self-respect was more important to me than a few dollars. He took the money, shook my hand and we never talked about it again. *He* learned something good about his son, and *I* learned something good about my father. And that *was* worth more than those few dollars I laid before him on our dinner table.

The next week, after I quit that fake job, telling the surprised, white-haired old druggist that I would *not* work for him anymore, unless he thought I was good enough to pay me from his own pocket, he offered me a real job on the spot, and I worked for him for the next six months.

After that, an old grade school friend, Rick Munden, who attended Bowen High School, some miles south of my neighborhood, persuaded me to join him in opening a newspaper stand during the summer after our freshman year. He told me it would be a great opportunity for me to check thousands of coins every day and really improve the value of my collection. I naively believed him. Together, we opened that newsstand in Hyde Park on August 21, 1965, making us both self-employed at fifteen. I figured at best, it would last just that one summer.

Except Rick decided to sell his fifty-per cent share to me fourteen months later, so he could have an actual life and not work seven-days-a-week, while I ended up staying on that corner for *twenty years.*

The worst part is that the only coin of any significant value found there in all that time, a rare 1909 VDB Lincoln cent, was found, and kept, by Rick during the short period of our partnership.

Then *he* went off to explore Afghanistan, Turkey, Malaysia and Australia, live on a boat in the Caribbean for nine years, work on the Hubble Telescope and more cool stuff like that, while I froze and boiled for decades at that damn newsstand.

I have to talk to him about that sometime.

But that's another story.

I think you may be amused at the conclusion of *this* story, about The Thousand Dollar Bill, in the meantime.

****

Three years later, while my father and I continued to struggle to keep going—my trying to make the newsstand a success with its very tiny percentage of profit per newspaper while going full time to the private school, and he trying to survive the surprisingly cutthroat world of selling insurance for The Equitable—I received a call at my apartment that my dad and I still shared in Hyde Park.

It was the umpteenth call from the Bursar's Office at the University of Chicago, trying to collect the tuition money that I *still* owed them, because I was *still* attending the Laboratory School, which was much better suited to wealthy Doctor's and Lawyer's kids than just-barely-making-it families, like mine.

But boy, did I hate those endless calls from some persistent whiny voice demanding that I better pay up or I would *not* be allowed to graduate. That diploma was becoming like some exotic rare perfume, to be paid for by the ounce.

Finally, about a month before my graduation in June 1968, my newsstand had grown successful enough that I was able to put together the thousand bucks I owed to the Whiny Voice. But before I did that, I decided to make a kind of *"statement"*, to reflect my four years of frustration and antagonism with my endless shortage of cash to pay them…and everyone else.

But first, to be fair to the University of Chicago and its thousands of hardworking employees, I always knew that they were all just trying to do their jobs, that it wasn't personal, that I always could have left that elite school and risked my life by attending the free, public, and gun-toting Hyde Park High a couple of dangerous blocks away. No one forced me to go the Lab School. I know, of course that if *nobody* paid their tuition, there'd be no Lab School.

But Readers, that's the sane, mature and rational voice of the fifty-six year-old man writing this story.

The vengeance-bent, eighteen year-old me was somewhat *less* generous in spirit.

This story that now follows is what I did to fully express my 'inner child', after four years of receiving irritating phone calls trying to get me to pay up my delinquent tuition.

Oh, I paid up, alright.

My way.

I went to my bank where I'd deposited all my newsstand money for the last three years, and spoke to Jack, a senior banker I knew. I was friendly with everyone there, flirted with all the very attractive tellers, the female ones, and knew many of the employees who worked there, who also were regular customers at my newsstand. I had a pretty good overall relationship with the bank.

So when I asked my friendly banker for a small favor, such as: Would he please cash my personal check for one thousand dollars with...*a one thousand dollar bill*?

He smiled, hesitated for a minute, and then said he'd see if he could find one for me in the vault. I was counting on his impish sense of humor, hoping it would make him want to help me. He never asked what it was to be used for.

In those days, the only use for thousand dollar bills was for bank-to-bank transactions. Today, it would all be done by electronic transfer with no paper involved at all. The average customer of a bank, *any* bank, as my friendly banker informed me, *never, ever,* saw currency like that or even knew denominations that large even existed.

But I'd been a serious coin collector since 1961, and knew all about American paper money, why our dollars were called *greenbacks,* how the Spanish *real* preceded the American dollar as the common coin of the realm in Colonial times, what the words *two-bits* really means, where the term *saw buck* came from, why the South was called Dixie, and why Davy Crockett ended up dying at the Alamo after he and President Andrew Jackson parted ways over United States monetary policy, and then Jackson refused to back Crockett in his third run as a U.S. Representative from Tennessee. I even knew where the word *dollar* came from.

And lastly, that the 1909 VDB Lincoln cent found by Rick Munden

Series 1934 One Thousand Dollar Bill

AUTHOR'S NOTE

A present day younger reader of my story might logically say, "So, what's the big deal? It's only a $1,000. That's no big deal in 2006." That, Reader, would be correct, except that in 1968, $1,000 would be the equivalent, due to inflation and a currently falling dollar, of about $5,000 today, which to me, at fifty-six, is still a lot of money.

This story will make more sense to a younger generation, if they understand that in 1968, a person could buy a brand-new sleek *Ford Mustang*, with a 351-engine, power disc brakes and steering, with a 3-speed automatic transmission...for about $3,500.

In other words, in 1968, for a thousand smackers, a kid could buy about a third of a *very* hot new car. Gas was about a quarter a gallon. A big bar of *Hershey's Chocolate*, with almonds, was a dime. A *Sunday Chicago Tribune* was twenty cents. *Playboy Magazine* was seventy-five cents. A guy could bribe a cop with ten bucks to help him forget about a speeding ticket.

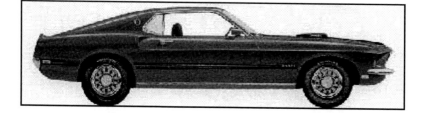

during his brief experience as a newsvendor, was designed by Victor David Brenner, after he was chosen to do that by President Theodore Roosevelt. And *chosen* is the right word, in Brenner's case.

Or to put it another way, the most widely minted and distributed coin in all the world's history of coinage, the Lincoln Penny, was designed by a Lithuanian Jew, someone just like me.

So unlike the average person, I *did* know thousand dollar bills existed and that former President Grover S. Cleveland's picture was smack in the center of each one.

When Bill the banker returned half an hour later with that so rarely seen bill, in a crisp white bank envelope, I thanked him, shook hands with him, and headed toward the Bursar's Office.

After all, they were waiting for me.

****

I found a parking place, located the Bursars Office and took my place in line, like the many dozens of other delinquent students whose degrees were also being held hostage. I saw that there were a good number of old fashioned bank teller type windows where a person would pay their fees. They had big, old, metal cash registers sitting on the heavy gray marble counters, too.

The room was packed with a great many last minute debt-payers that warm May day in 1968, yet it was also very dignified and silent at the same time. Paying debts does not make very many people want to sing and dance. Most students just meekly and patiently waited in the slow-moving lines until it was their turn to *pay-the-piper*.

As I looked from window to window, I saw that the *pipers* in this place were mostly quiet and quite serious middle-aged, no-nonsense women, endlessly ringing up the rivers of fives, tens, twenties and fifty dollar bills flowing in toward them, and then robotically sliding the change back to the students on those same cold marble counters.

While I waited in that long line for *my* turn to come, slowly getting closer to my teller, I turned to look around the room and accidentally bumped into an older university student, about twenty, standing behind me. I apologized and for no reason in particular, mentioned to him in a very quiet voice that I was going to pay my tuition with a thousand dollar bill. I guess I thought it would make him smile, or something.

Maybe I was bored or figured it was no big deal after all, and the teller would simply take my money, give me my two dollars and fifty cents change and then snap in a weary voice:

"NEXT!"

But that "worldly and sophisticated" university student regarded me with as much attention as he would an annoying and noisy tea kettle, and he went back to reading his Kurt Vonnegut paperback, without responding to me.

I shrugged at his indifference to me, turned back around and found that it was indeed my turn at the window to pay off my tuition, after my four endless years of attending school there. So, I pulled a letter from my back pants pocket that stated exactly how much I owed, which was $997.50, complete with my student ID number. Then I pulled that crisp bank envelope from a chest pocket in my shirt, where I felt it would be safer.

As the bored older woman on the other side of the teller's window waited expectantly for a check from me, or a fat wad of fifty twenties, or some other routine combination of common currency, I calmly and quietly slid my very clean and seldom circulated...one thousand dollar bill...across the counter toward the woman and said, in a polite, yet firm voice,

"May I have my change...*and*...a receipt, please?"

There was a momentary pause, as the teller focused her weary eyes on the alien currency laying there before her. As the seconds crawled past, and the teller didn't move, the bored and snotty university guy behind me looked over my shoulder in annoyed impatience, to see what could *possibly* be the delay. Then he let out a startled gasp, and said, much too loudly,

"*Oh my God! It really is...a thousand dollar bill!*"

The teller snapped out of her catatonic fixation on the rarely seen bill laying before her and slowly looked up at me. Then I heard a sudden rustling and shuffling of many feet. I turned my head to see why and saw about a hundred newly fascinated students break from their neat and orderly lines and surge over to where I was quietly waiting for my change...*and* a receipt, to see something that, most likely, none of them had ever seen before.

The room ceased to be a quiet and solemn Temple of Money.

Now, to my delight, it was becoming a freak show.

And the many voices now filling the room said, ever louder:

"*My goodness, where did he ever get it?*"

"*Oh, that couldn't possibly be real money. It must be a joke.*"

"*Jesus, man! That's a lot of damn bread in one piece of paper!*"

"*Hey, whose picture's on it? Scrooge McDuck?*"

"*I bet they arrest the kid if it's a phony...*"

"*Hey, man, how many joints can ya buy with a grand?*"

The stunned teller picked up the bill and turned to the left in her cubicle, then somewhat confused, turned to the right, as the babble in the room grew in volume. Then she turned around as her irritated boss pushed through the little mob of tellers from all the other windows, because they all *had* to see…*The Thousand Dollar Bill.*

No one…was paying their tuition.

No one…was waiting in line.

No one…was doing anything except gawking at…

The Thousand Dollar Bill.

The very annoyed and self-important teller's boss, in his *proper vest* and university tie, said to me in his most antagonized and condescending voice, that I'm certain was a curse for the poor tellers working there,

"Just exactly *where* did you get this denomination from, kid? What do you think you're trying to pull here? You think we're all idiots?"

But I gently responded to him, with real amazement in my voice.

"Oh, haven't you *ever* seen one of those before? Gosh, I didn't think it was any big deal. You could always call my bank. Here's the number. Ask for Bill. Can I have my change please? And a receipt? I don't want to be late for my German class."

And I smiled sweetly at the pompous bag of wind in his *Proper Vest.*

It *is* important to *always* be polite.

Especially…if it drives the other person…*crazy.*

Then the *Proper Vest* grabbed the bill from the teller and turned abruptly to the left to see if any of his tellers had ever seen a bill *that* large.

Nobody had.

Then he turned to the right and asked the tellers and managers crowding in there if any of *them* could verify the authenticity of…*The Thousand Dollar Bill.*

Nobody could.

Finally, he turned and focused his icy glare at me. Because *I knew* and I'm sure *he knew,* too, that it would be illegal for him to refuse to accept real United States currency for the payment of a legitimate debt. Even if there were no place to put it in his cash register. Even if it really pissed off the *Proper Vest* that I had disrupted the perfect order of the *Money Changers* in this *Temple of Knowledge.*

Except he had no idea if it was real money or just some scam I was trying to pull on the university. Because the *Proper Vest* had *never seen*…*a Thousand Dollar Bill* before. And I was…*so sorry*…about that.

He ought to get out more, and learn new things.

Then tightly clutching the bill and also the phone number of my banker friend, the *Proper Vest* went to find a phone to call my bank and teach me a *real* lesson as he called my bluff, damn it. No bank would give that kind of money to a miserable teenaged punk like me. Why, I wasn't even old enough to buy a beer. Well, he certainly had me *now*, didn't he?

All the many students in that Bursar's Office waited in excited anticipation to see if I would either get change for a thousand dollars....or....get arrested.

I heard someone ask: "Who was Grover Cleveland?"

The crowded room was in a state of suspended animation. I guess they didn't have too many cliff-hangers in the university's Bursar's Office.

Minutes clicked by.

Then, suddenly, the *Proper Vest* reappeared.

Not happy.

Not happy at all.

He sternly instructed my teller:

"Give him his change. The rest of you clerks get back to your windows and process all these other people. I mean *NOW!*"

But I piped up, the soul of wounded innocence,

"*And* my receipt, too."

The *Proper Vest* glared at me, very annoyed at my smart-aleck attitude, I guess.

"*What* did you say? *What's* your problem, kid?"

I responded, a bit less generously.

"I *said...I* want my *change...and* my *receipt. Now!*

"You know, mister, you really ought to wait on people faster here.

"Maybe...the university needs a *new* manager in the Bursar's Office."

The *Proper Vest* stomped over to the register between the two of us. He angrily punched the register's metal keys, one after the other, until the register drawer popped opened with a mechanical ring. He snatched out two one dollar bills and two quarters, slapped them all on the counter and pushed them over to me.

I waited.

Then he ripped off the paper receipt that stuck out of the top of the register, like a long, teasing, white tongue, waving at him, and slapped *that* down on the counter and over to me, as well.

"Thank you...*Sir*," I said, but he was already gone.

It is *very* important to always be polite.

It is what separates us from the animals.

And I left that crowded Bursar's Office knowing that they would *never* call me again.

Ever.

****

Epilogue

Two years later, in Spring 1970, I was selling newspapers, as usual, during the evening rush hour, in front of my old, wooden, weather-beaten, Hyde Park newspaper stand, by now universally called *Bob's Newsstand*, when an older gentleman approached me to buy a newspaper. He seemed to me to have a permanently serious expression etched onto his face.

He was very neatly dressed in a conservative black business suit, his tie knotted just so, his rimless glasses perched perfectly on the end of his nose—maybe just a tad...prissy. He was perhaps in his mid-sixties, slender and about five feet five inches tall.

He requested a *Chicago Tribune*, which I swiftly folded in half with one hand and tucked under his arm, in a single unbroken motion. Then, as I was giving him the change for his dollar, looking down for a moment at the coins I was pulling out from the ancient canvas change belt tied around my waist, I heard him say, with a small gasp:

"It's...*you!*"

I looked up at him, distracted from what I was doing, not yet comprehending his surprising and accusing tone.

"It's...*me?*" I responded, warily.

He continued with an unexpectedly emotional torrent of words.

"*You're* that damn kid that came to the university's Bursar's Office that day with the...the...*Thousand Dollar Bill*...to pay your tuition!"

I stared at him, silently.

But he went on, snarling at me on the street, in front of my newsstand.

"*Because of you, all* the tellers from *all* the other cages rushed over to see something they never saw before! The dozens of students waiting in all the other lines to pay their tuition crowded around the teller cage *you* were standing at, to see the same damn thing!

"*Everything* in that busy office came to a halt. *All* work stopped. *Nobody* answered the phones. *No* money was collected. That day was just a *disaster.*

"All because of you, and your *damned...Thousand Dollar Bill!*

"Never had there been a more disruptive incident in all the thirty years I worked in that office! Did you *ever* stop to consider exactly how *much* trouble you caused us that day?"

Deeply moved by his story, there were tears in my eyes.

I reached over and grasped the antagonized little man's right hand. I shook it warmly, as he stood there *totally* dumbfounded by my unexpected reaction to his ranting. I smiled sweetly at him and said,

"I think that's just the *nicest* thing…*anyone*…has *ever* said to me!"

He jerked his hand away from mine and backed up a step, clutching his newspaper, ignoring his change, staring at me all the while, the way a sane person might respond toward someone who was unpredictably demented.

Then he sputtered at me,

"You're…you're…*out of your mind!*"

I looked at him, soulfully, nodding in agreement with him, and responded…just a *bit* too loudly,

"Could be…"

That frantic little man swiftly retreated from my newsstand, never taking his startled eyes off of me, stumbling backwards until he suddenly collided into the trunk of his parked car. He quickly picked up his fallen car keys, his newspaper, dove into the driver's seat and roared off into the evening rush hour traffic.

He seemed *so* upset.

I was so…*pleased.*

Maybe…maybe I'll go back and visit that Bursar's Office myself, one day, just to see if anyone *else* there remembers me?

That could be *very* interesting.

It sure is…*nice*…to be remembered.

Me and Grover...we go waaay back!

This page
intentionally
left blank

He became apoplectic with rage and frustration, calling me a little bastard and a troublemaker, and that I would remain in the giant, empty mess hall until I finished every drop of my ravioli sauce. He glanced at the big clock hanging high up on the wall, over the windows. It read 12:30 p.m. Then, his angry eyes bulging down at me, he told me that there would be no dinner for me at 5 p.m. unless I finished all the ravioli sauce.

I said nothing more to him, remaining where I was standing by my place at the table. He angrily stomped out of the mess hall, slamming the heavy door as he left.

It was very quiet in that big room with all the people gone. Just me and the big clock, ticking away. After a little while, I sat down at my cabin's table, looked at my miserable, almost empty plate, and I pushed it way from me, across the table.

I sat there, as the minutes slowly passed, very silent in my determination to defy that stupid and cruel adult. He thought he could make a little boy crumble in fear and submit to his sinister rage.

He was very wrong, this time.

I would wait.

4

The Chocolate Frosting Conspiracy

I've written numerous stories in my previous books about conflict, rebellion, determination, defeat, self-respect and expulsion. The earliest of those stories started in 1958, when I was eight years old, involving learning about my family in Europe and their fate in the Holocaust during World War II.

But recently, I was thinking about: When does a person begin to become who they will eventually be? How does that process work? Who was the most significant influence? Finally, who was part of a one-time but unforgettable incident that perhaps made the other pieces of a person's developing personality fall into place?

Some moments might occur when you are in a classroom, or in a crowd somewhere. Some, when you are with your extended family in various settings and combinations. Some moments might happen when you are at work or in a church or synagogue. And some moments may happen when you believe that you are completely alone, even if you don't know that really, you are not.

Like this incident involving an angry confrontation between un-equals that left the beginnings of a crystallization in the mind of a little boy about looking at a seemingly unsolvable dilemma and then learning to accept the possibility that another person, even a total stranger, could show him the way out.

****

In August 1959, I was sent to my first sleep-over summer camp, located "somewhere in the rural Midwestern United States." This was my first time away from my home on the South Side of Chicago, for more than a single night. It was for *sixty* days.

I was sent there from a violent and unhappy home where there was friction between my parents all the time. Screaming and metal objects could fill the air at any moment. It was a perfect example of two miserable people choosing to stay together for "the sake of the children," whatever those words mean. A tragically flawed concept.

This dangerous atmosphere caused me to become wary and untrusting of most adults about not yielding to what I felt were unreasonable demands from some person outside of my family: grade school teachers, Hebrew school teachers, and especially, gym coaches seeking that I be part of a group learning to play baseball, football or basketball.

"Unreasonable demands" became my very broad definition of almost every authority figure who sought my cooperation in following set rules, including even the patrol boy near my house who insisted that I stop and wait before crossing the street on my way to school, until *he* determined that it was safe for me to cross.

I decided, after we first met, that he was being arbitrary about when he would allow me to cross the street, and that he was filled with the *power of his post*. But I refused to recognize his authority... hundreds and hundreds of times.

Then he would report me to some disciplinarian figure in my school, the righteous little snot, and that would lead to my being prevented from going to recess that day, or gym class, or the library, or some other privilege being taken away from me as punishment for my violation of the street crossing rules. Hundreds and hundreds of times.

That particular patrol boy did not grasp that nothing he could do to me would force me to recognize his power over me. His constant reporting of my choosing to cross the street that he guarded... whenever I felt like it...without his permission, did not enhance his standing in my mind.

Even though I repeatedly lost privileges, year after year, I would not submit to what I felt were rules, and an enforcer, I considered to be ridiculous. I was tenacious, determined and very, very stubborn.

So my parents placing me in a twenty-four hour situation, for sixty days, where every single adult that I met was authorized to tell me what I could or could not do, was not a plan made in heaven. That and the fact that I was allergic to just about every other plant growing in the Midwestern countryside, causing me to sneeze and itch constantly, did not improve my attitude.

When to get up. When to eat. When to hike. When to swim or play some dumb game. When to sleep. When to talk and when to shut up. That camp, its counselors and I...were not a good fit. I didn't want to be there. I just wanted to be left alone.

Then came:

The Ravioli Incident.

Every day in this cavernous metal mess hall—that seemed to me to be the size of an aircraft hanger—were assembled hundreds of noisy campers assigned to dozens of tables, three times a day, each presided over by a counselor or a C.I.T. (counselor-in-training) who would tell his campers when to say grace, when you could eat, how much you could eat and when you could leave the table. But *only* after the camper had eaten *every* scrap of food on his plate.

Forcing me, even at nine years old, into an intensely controlled situation like that was an invitation to a confrontation. By the fourth week into my sentence at that summer camp, it happened.

There were many counselors at the camp, some who were older teenagers and many who were adults of different ages. Most of them were friendly, cheerful people who wanted the summer camp experience to be happy and memorable.

Not at my table.

I had some Prussian Drill Officer who was so exacting and so unfriendly in his manner and language toward me that our daily contact was simply hell. One day, early in August 1959, ravioli was served as the main course at lunch, with no other choices. I was not fond of Italian food at that time, or very familiar with it either.

Besides things that grew in the countryside, I also had many food allergies and was very limited as to what I could eat without reacting. The wrong kind of food could constrict my breathing and make my esophagus swell up. Even today. But a person having allergies to many things in the world was still a new science and not yet taken seriously by the average person back in the ignorant Fifties. A resistance to my eating something could be misinterpreted by another person who did not realize the possibly serious consequences to me. Or believe me if I tried to explain my situation to him.

The other problem with my having so many allergies was that they made me different than many other kids at that time, not in a good way, and with my already contentious nature I didn't want to call even more negative attention to myself. So my fragile condition was something I didn't talk about.

Those little soft white squares of dough, with their crimped edges and mysterious contents inside, swimming in a thick red sauce were not especially appealing to me. My Polish and Lithuanian grandmothers didn't cook food like that for me to eat.

But I was very hungry from the morning's activities, including a long hike, and I had to eat *something*. When the large white serving bowl of ravioli came around to me, I hesitated, not sure whether to chance this strange new kind of food, or not.

After about fifteen seconds, the Nazi at the head of my table ordered me to take some food and pass on the bowl. He sounded angry and intimidated most of the campers in my cabin. The previous week, he responded to something I asked him by saying that I asked the stupidest questions that he had ever heard. He seemed to relish making embarrassing comments about a kid only when there were other people around, to deepen the wound.

When we were supposed to send postcards home, periodically, telling our parents what a wonderful time we were having, I wrote a card telling them that I hated the camp and wanted them to come get me.

My parents never received that postcard.

My counselor read every postcard, tore up the ones that did not meet his approval and then sent his own postcard saying:

"Dear Mom and Dad, I am having a great time. Love..."

and then he would sign the name of the offending camper. I was not aware that this was happening until another camper discovered him doing this late one night and told me about it. It was supposed to be a secret. I saw that this man would write lies on a card, like I was his helpless prisoner. When I confronted my counselor about it, he called me a liar, among other nasty things, in front of all the other kids in my cabin.

The next week, he wrote out my required postcard, when I refused to write one, right in front of me — with a sneer, like *what was I gonna do about it* — and then signed my name. It was a frightening moment for me. It seems hard for me today to believe such a thing could have happened, but it did.

So when this evil soul ordered me to eat, I meekly submitted to his will, and placed one large serving on my plate and then passed on the bowl. The other campers snickered.

I tentatively lifted one of the little squares of ravioli with my fork, and nibbled at the edge of it. It wasn't very good, but not completely horrible either, so I ate it. But first, I scraped off all the thick, red sauce, which *was* horrible. Then I finished all the ravioli remaining on my plate.

When the bell rang and lunch was over, everyone slid off their seat to leave the mess hall, including me, when my counselor barked at me saying that I had to finish all the food on my plate before I could leave the table. I looked at him in disbelief and told him that I did, that I ate every piece of ravioli that I had taken from the serving bowl.

But he snapped right back at me that I hadn't eaten all the tomato

My sister, Bonnie, 11, and me, 9, at sleep-over camp, "somewhere in the rural Midwestern United States" in Summer 1959.

sauce. I responded that I didn't like the sauce and I didn't want it. In a mocking tone of voice, he reminded me that I had to eat *everything* on my plate because that was the camp rule.

I refused to eat it.

He placed a spoon on my plate and ordered me to eat every speck of it or stay in that mess hall until I did eat it. All of this was said loudly enough for all the other hundreds of campers in the mess hall to hear. Many of them turned to look at me. Some of them pointed and laughed.

I decided right then that I had had enough of this belligerent jerk. I turned to face him, looked up at him and simply said,

"No."

My counselor's face darkened. He roared at all the other campers to leave, *now!*

Soon the mess hall was empty except for the two of us and my lonely plate of lousy ravioli sauce.

The man stood very close to me and said, again,

"Eat it."

I remained where I was standing and quietly said again,

"No."

He became apoplectic with rage and frustration, calling me a little bastard and a troublemaker, and that I would remain in the giant, empty mess hall until I finished *every* drop of my ravioli sauce. He glanced at the big clock hanging high up on the wall, over the windows. It read 12:30 p.m. Then, his angry eyes bulging down at me, he told me that there would be no dinner for me at 5 p.m. unless I finished all the ravioli sauce.

I said nothing more to him, remaining where I was standing by my place at the table. He angrily stomped out of the mess hall, slamming the heavy door as he left.

It was very quiet in that big room with all the people gone. Just me and the big clock, ticking away. After a little while, I sat down at my cabin's table, looked at my miserable, almost empty plate, and I pushed it way from me, across the table.

I sat there, as the minutes slowly passed, very silent in my determination to defy that stupid and cruel adult. He thought he could make a little boy crumble in fear and submit to his sinister rage.

He was very wrong, this time.

I would wait.

I had encountered other people like him in my young life, and I lived with one, too. But when you're branded, as I was very early on, as a troublesome, angry and uncooperative child, that title travels with you from teacher to teacher, grade to grade, through the years.

No adult would listen to or believe anything that I would say to them because I was an established *Pain-In-The-Ass*. Once you win that title, it is *yours*, and no one can take it away.

But even at nine, I knew right from wrong, good from bad---and I was right and he was wrong. And bad, too.

So I sat there.

Time went by.

1 p.m....
2 p.m....
3 p.m....

I thought I was alone, when I saw a face peek out at me from a door far away at the end of the mess hall, where the kitchen was. Then the door opened.

A very large black woman—the camp cook—stood by the door and stared at me.

She smiled.

I didn't.

She was tall, large-breasted, with wide hips, very dark skin and strong arms, dressed in a white uniform buttoned up the front. I guess she must have liked her own cooking, even if I didn't. She had kind eyes and a friendly face. I could see quite clearly from that far away, forty-seven years ago.

She slowly walked toward me, occasionally looking at that big clock high up on the wall, and then back at me. It was 3:30 p.m.

Before 1959, people with dark brown skin like hers were called *colored.* Then some time later they were called *negroes.* Some time after that, *black.* Today I believe the politically correct designation is *African-American.* But in time, that may change.

For my story, written in 2006, I'll just call her: the Cook.

When the Cook stood opposite me on the other side of the table where I was sitting, resolute in my defiance, she smiled down at me and said,

"Child, what's your name?"

I responded, begrudgingly, considering her to be part of the enemy,

"Bobby."

"Bobby," she replied, "why don't you just eat up that little bit of sauce and go run outside and play? I heard that whole evil thing that man said to you, and I think you shouldn't have to stay cooped up in here."

Surprised by her gentleness and warm tone of voice, I nevertheless responded,

"I *won't* eat it. It's just awful and that man can't make me do it."

She listened and regarded me for a moment, her head tilted to the side, considering. Then she spoke again, quietly, and asked me,

"So you're going to let that nasty man make you stay in here, all alone, because of some cold ravioli sauce?"

"No," I answered, looking up at her, unused to having an adult willingly listen to what I had to say. "I'm staying in here...because I won't let that nasty man *win.*"

My answer caused a different reaction on her face, a kind of stiffening that I didn't understand in 1959. She nodded to me, turned and glanced over at that big clock and returned to the kitchen. It was ten to four.

Time passed.

I sat there.

Then at 4:30 p.m., the big kitchen door suddenly swung open and the Cook stood there, filling the doorway with her big self in her white uniform and her dark brown skin, mixing something in a large green bowl with a wooden spoon.

"Hey, Bobby," she yelled out to me, snapping me out of my gloomy daydreams. "Run over here, child. I want to show you something.

"And bring that lunch plate with you, too."

Then she turned and went back inside, letting the kitchen door swing shut behind her.

Surprised and very curious, I stood up, grabbed my plate and ran over to the kitchen door. I slowly pushed the heavy door open with my shoulder, careful not to spill any sauce off of the plate. The Cook was standing there, next to a steaming sink in a room with enormous windows, completely filled with heavy metal pots, pans, plates, glasses, trays and silverware. There wasn't much room to run around in her kitchen, and the smiling Cook filled a good part of that small space.

She was still stirring something in that big green bowl, too. She motioned me to come over to her and look into the bowl. I cautiously edged over to her and she lowered the bowl for me to see.

It was filled, almost to the top with...*thick*...*dark*...*creamy*...chocolate frosting. It smelled *so* good, and the moist kitchen air was thick with the aroma of warm cocoa. There were a number of cakes sitting on the stove behind her, waiting to be covered with the wonderful frosting.

This was long before my chocolate addiction was something I was aware of.

I looked up at the Cook, clutching my plate with its cold ravioli sauce, waiting for her to speak. She smiled a wide smile, bright with many white teeth. Even though we were the only people in that vast building, she whispered, in an *I've got a secret* voice:

"Bobby, I'll make you a deal."

She reached behind her for something. It was a clear glass of water with a teaspoon sitting in it.

"Take this little spoon and eat just one spoonful of that ravioli sauce. Then, very fast, drink down this glass of cold water. You'll barely taste the sauce."

The Cook smiled, her eyes dancing.

"If you do this for me, I'll let you take one finger and scoop out as much of this chocolate frosting as your finger can hold. Then, when that nasty man asks me if you ate up the tomato sauce, an' he will, too, I can look him straight in the eye, without lyin', and say,

"Why, yes. He most *certainly* did.

"I just won't say *how much!*"

I couldn't believe this.

A choice.

It was up to *me* to decide what I wanted to do.

There was something else to her offer besides the ravioli sauce and the chocolate, but at the age of nine, I was too young to understand it. But I sensed that it was more important than the ravioli sauce…to the Cook.

I wanted that chocolate frosting.

Bad.

I wanted to please the Cook.

And most of all, I wanted to get out of that mess hall.

I nodded to her, smiling for the first time, knowing a good deal when it was offered to me. I grabbed the teaspoon, scooped up some of the cold red sauce, braced myself and then dumped it into my mouth, trying to miss my tongue, letting it fall down my throat. Then the cook swiftly held out the glass of water to me and I quickly drank it all down at once, letting the flood of cold water wash away the terrible flavor I said I'd never eat. Water overflowed my small mouth and soaked the front of my T-shirt.

The Cook took the plate from my hand and placed it under the open faucet in the sink, hot steaming water pouring out of it, and I watched as she let the water wash my lunch plate clean, until the last bit of the red poison flowed down the drain. She turned off the water.

Then with her two strong black hands, the Cook held the bowl of chocolate frosting in front of her, honoring her part of the deal. Careful to use only one finger—my strongest one—I scooped down deep into the mixing bowl and came out with a huge sticky mass of frosting.

With my head tilted back, I held that finger right over my wide open mouth, and just let the chocolate frosting fall.

And fall.

And fall.

Oh God, it was… *fabulous!*

The Cook handed me a wet towel to wipe off my sticky face and hide the evidence of our secret rebellion.

I spontaneously hugged her, throwing my slender arms as far around her as I could. Surprised, but without saying a word, she too wrapped her huge, strong arms around me—like a protective mother hen with her wayward chick—and she hugged me back. I can still feel the warmth of her body, decades later.

Then she said to me, still whispering conspiratorially,

"Now you best run along before someone sees you in here. I don't want no trouble for you...an' me neither."

She held open the big door to the kitchen so I could race out of the building, and when I looked back at her, just before escaping that prison, I heard her call out to me,

"Now, don't you tell *no one* about this, child, you hear me?"

But I could see she was laughing, while she said it.

****

In the nearly fifty years since I ran out of that enormous mess hall, I have never before today told a soul about my secret deal with the Cook.

Not to the few friends I had in that camp.

Not to my older sister, Bonnie, who was also there in the camp, in the girl's dorm.

Not to my parents when I finally came home, one month later.

Not to any of my life-long friends, in the decades still to come since that grim day.

Not even to my wife of thirty years, Joyce.

I promised not to tell anyone...and I didn't.

****

Not very long ago, I was reading a small item in the business section of my local newspaper. It mentioned that my old camp from 1959, with its many wooded acres, had recently been sold for a significant sum to a real estate development company by the heirs of the now deceased original owners of that camp.

I decided, after letting that news item sink in, that at last I was free to break my silence about that wonderful Cook, who made such a difference in a tough situation, so long ago. I wrote this story in Traverse City, Michigan over the July 4, 2006 holiday weekend, while my kids were playing on a long sandy beach running along the Traverse City Bay. My wife was sitting in the shade reading her latest summer mystery and watching the children play.

About one hundred yards away from them, I found a quiet spot where I could write this story, on a weathered picnic table off by itself, under some ancient leafy trees. After a while, I realized that some people might smile when they first read the title I gave to this incident, **The Chocolate Frosting Conspiracy,** mistakenly assuming that it was in some way...funny.

But to me, the title is just plain fact. I soon discovered that my pain, anger and resentment toward the cruel man from the Summer of '59 was still buried deep within me, when silently I took myself far back in time...to do my best to write about those ancient moments *exactly* as they really happened.

It didn't take long for me to get up and turn the heavy wooden picnic table around to face the trees, away from some vacationing couple's curious glance, so they wouldn't be able to see a fifty-six year-old man...finally...crying a nine year-old boy's tears.

****

And so I learned something from that wonderful woman.
Sometimes you fight.
Sometimes you win.
Sometimes you lose.

And sometimes, you find a middle-ground you can live with.
Not a perfect world, but a lot better than the one I was living in. I learned all that from the beautiful Cook with her big smile, and her solid-gold heart.

And, that big bowl of…*thick…dark…creamy…chocolate…frosting.*

I learned you can concede sometimes, about something, and still keep your dignity. No small concept to learn when you are just nine years old.

I even…don't repeat this…I even was a patrol boy for a short time, in 1963.

It didn't kill me, either.

People can change.

This page
intentionally
left blank

**Rabbi Jonathan Magidovitch of
Congregation B'nai Torah
in Highland Park, Illinois**

Introduction and Insight into the Origins of
A Child's Holocaust Story

I guess after a person realizes that he's a storyteller, eventually even his stories have stories. Like this one, for example. Follow the genesis (an appropriate choice of words, in this case) of how the following grim story, *A Child's Holocaust Story*, came to be written.

My wife, Joy, and I belong to a very enlightened synagogue, Congregation B'nai Torah, located on a bluff overlooking Lake Michigan in Highland Park, Illinois. We first noticed it—tucked away as it is from almost all traffic patterns—when my sister, Bonnie, was married there a number of years ago.

We first met the rabbi there, Jonathan Magidovitch, a relatively young person, it seemed to me, when he officiated at Bonnie's ceremony in a lively, humorous way, but still taking the moment seriously and, at all times, maintaining a very Jewish flavor to everything he said.

I was impressed. The synagogue was and is a beehive of activity, and Rabbi Jonathan has his hands full trying to keep the diverse groups using the facilities—all at the same time—from trampling each other as they rush from room to room. There are many classes for adults, children and converts.

There is a level or originality and enthusiasm in this synagogue that was refreshing to me, and Joyce, too, that we hadn't encountered elsewhere. We decided to join and try it out. I gradually became involved in several of its programs—something that I had never done at any other synagogue I'd belonged to in the prior forty-plus years. My interest surprised even me. I was learning new things, going to Friday Sabbath services more often than ever before. It wasn't like an obligation and often, it was *fun*. That was not a word I would have ever attached to any synagogue I had been part of, beginning in 1958.

After being there awhile and getting to know other congregants as well as Rabbi Jonathan, we enrolled our youngest daughter, Sarah, now ten, in B'nai Torah's Hebrew School. We enjoyed the Friday Shabbat services and other events we attended at our new temple. I also began to learn—I heard many of Rabbi Jonathan's sermons, written and delivered in a refreshing way—that he had a nimble mind and a generosity of spirit toward the wide range of how Jews sought to be Jews. His lines weren't rigid. All thoughts were welcome. I found Rabbi Jonathan to be, well...*ecclesiastically elastic.*

And the world turned...

If you have just read another story in this book, *The Foreclosure Quintet*, you'll already know that my life has been an economic rollercoaster. If you *haven't* read it, stop here, do not pass go, do not collect $200, and go back and read it first.

During one grimly miserable period of uncertainty and insecurity about how I would make a living, I decided that the new temple in our lives was a beloved luxury that was simply beyond our ability to pay for membership and schooling for Sarah.

I made an appointment to talk to Rabbi Jonathan about how things were and how I felt about it, and then told him maybe the best thing would be that my family should leave, since we couldn't pay our way, and that we didn't want to be a burden to such a great place.

Rabbi Jonathan listened intently, as always, alert but quiet. But when I brought up the last part about leaving B'nai Torah, he suddenly broke in and said, flatly,

"If you leave, we'll hunt you down and bring you back."

Not expecting such a non-rabbinic response, I was momentarily speechless—an uncommon condition as anyone who knows me would swear to. I wasn't prepared for words like those. When I said nothing in response, he continued.

"There are people in this congregation, prosperous people, who have made provisions for people in situations like yours, and your being here is more important than whether you can pay or not, at this time. You already contribute to this temple in other important ways. Money is not the only way we value our members."

There were many things that Rabbi Jonathan could have chosen to say. He could have wished me luck. He could have said he would have to talk to the membership committee to see if there was some way we could continue to belong there. He *could* have said the expected things like that; but instead, the words he did choose to say, and the intensity of the way he said them was so unexpected and so, well, uplifting to my spirits at a time of so much misery, that they instantly became etched on a plaque in my memory as an example of a man who is perfectly matched to his work.

Too moved to respond—then and now—I smiled, thanked him and left.

Time went by.

One day, Joy and I were having chapter eighty-six of an ongoing argument about something. It was a simmering, low level annoyance, but seemingly irresolvable. I won't describe it; but my wife is a smart girl. She called me one day and asked me if I would be willing to go with her to a consulting session in the Rabbi's office, to see if we could find some reasonable solution to our frustrating bickering.

Well, never in my life had I ever considered such a thing. It had never occurred to me that rabbis were trained to help couples in distress. Weddings, funerals, bar mitzvahs, yeah, sure. But mediating grief between a couple? I didn't know that was part of their job. I told Joyce I'd think about it. This was very personal stuff. I was uncertain about what to do. Then I reached a decision.

I told Joy that not only would I go with her, but also whatever Rabbi Jonathan felt was the fairest way to resolve things, I'd agree to it, even if it was against my position. I told her I was so impressed with her realization that the Rabbi was a fair, unbiased person to talk to—something beyond my imagination—and my respect for him was such that I would be confident his perspective would be the best way to go. Momentary silence. Joy asked if I was really serious after such a long period of our battling about this problem. I told her to set up the appointment and let's deal with it. I meant every word.

Most likely doubting me, Joy and I soon met with Rabbi Jonathan. As always, he listened intently, quietly, without interrupting. First Joy's side, then mine. We, too, were courteous toward each other, which was not a common condition when our dispute was in the air of our house. Then the Rabbi thought about it. We waited to see how this new experience would play out. He restated both our positions to see if what he heard was what we both felt. It was accurate. I was certain he would understand the correctness of my feelings and gently encourage Joy to change.

That's not what happened. Rabbi Jonathan saw our two different positions as on two different planes that did not intersect. What I wanted to happen and what Joy was doing were unconnected events, and regardless of whether I approved or not, in his opinion, she was not only doing the *right* thing, but also the most *compassionate* thing, as well.

His argument was so well-reasoned and so clear to me, that even though I essentially lost what I had hoped to achieve, there was no question in my mind that his advice was the only way to go. He made it clear that he shared my frustration, but that Joy was not the cause of it. I didn't say anything. Then, consulting his appointment calendar, he asked if we wanted to come see him next week to see if he could help us any further with this sensitive issue. But I spoke up and said,

"No. It won't be necessary. I told Joy before we came that I'd agree to whatever you recommended. And I will."

Then there was another one of those periodic silences that occur in my life, when people are surprised by one thing or another.

Joy didn't expect me to actually agree to do what I said I'd do, earlier. Her face reflected that. The Rabbi hadn't known about my prior offer to Joy. So, as the air of disbelief lingered a bit, I said,

"Really. I'm content. If that's what you think is fair, then there's nothing else to argue about. We'll find some other thing to bicker about, I expect."

With that, I pushed back my chair from his desk and helped Joy with her coat. We all shook hands and were getting ready to leave his office when the Rabbi spoke up and asked me,

"Bob...do you have a Holocaust story."

Not expecting that question in conjunction with my marital dispute visit—not expecting that question, period—I stopped leaving and turned to the Rabbi and replied, slowly,

"Well...yes, I do...I just don't want to write it."

The Rabbi knew I wrote stories and had recently self-published my first book.

He also had generously agreed to read a number of my stories before the book was published, and he had a pretty good idea of what I wrote about. And my style. My stories were autobiographical and wide ranging, but had a Jewish tilt to them.

The Rabbi responded, again unexpectedly,

"Well...would you write your Holocaust story...for me?"

A much different question.

Without any more hesitation, I immediately agreed, for the second time that morning. The temple was observing the annual Holocaust Remembrance Day, which is not in any way a holiday, but instead a determination not to forget what had happened to Jews as a people, and the many other powerless victims caught up in the horrors of the Nazi nightmare.

Rabbi Jonathan wanted to see what I'd come up with, and two weeks later, after some revisions, he approved of the final draft of the grim story about the fate of my family who never left Europe. He said he was very happy—if a person could say such a thing—about my offbeat perspective of what happened, and then he asked me if I would read it to the congregation on a Friday night in two weeks, after the Shabbat service. I said I would, but wondered to myself if I could really read it, out loud. I wanted to be known for my books and stories; but not all the stories I wrote were meant to be read by me to others.

I rehearsed reading the story with my patient (and newly victorious) wife, many times, hoping to make it all the way through without dissolving in tears. To do that, I had to remove some words that proved to be triggers and eventually felt I could do it, probably. Maybe. I had no idea what would happen.

On Friday, April 28, 2006, in front of about fifty people who only knew me as a familiar face from other Fridays, I read my story, *A Child's Holocaust Story*. At that time, very few people, any place, were aware that I was a writer, and had aspirations of doing it full time, if Fortune ever smiled on me. I managed to make it all the way through the ten pages, except for the very last line.

I thought it went well. Some people came up to me later and said they liked the story, and asked if I had written anything else?

So, maybe my complex Rabbi was doing more than simply asking me to write a Holocaust story.

It wouldn't be the first time.

If the following terrible story moves you, makes you think, makes you angry, helps you to learn about something virtually incomprehensible that happened so long ago you knew nothing about it, than Rabbi Jonathan Magidovitch found the right vessel to accomplish this purpose: To remind the world that we are still here...and always will be.

Although it was extraordinarily painful for me to write, still, I thank him for that.

*When I was very young...**too** young...I first heard the story from my Grandma Warman about the devastating **pogrom** that came to her small village of Dobra, just outside of Krakow, Poland, in 1916.*

A pogrom — a Russian word that means an organized massacre of a minority group, in this case, Jews — meant a hoard of Cossacks on huge horses would swoop down on a defenseless shtetl, or Jewish town, kill the men, rape the women and steal or kill the children. The anti-Semitic Austrian-Hungarian military authorities never interfered, and considered this a form of population control of a troublesome minority in their Empire.

5

A Child's Holocaust Story

Wyatt Earp of Arizona
and
Osher Katzman of Byelorussia

Wyatt Earp is buried in a Jewish cemetery near Los Angeles.

Too often it seems that some people learn just a little about a person's life, and then think they know all they need to know to judge that person.

Thirty seconds of deadly gunfire at the OK Corral on a dusty street in Tombstone, Arizona on October 26, 1881 is not enough information to define the entire life of a man who lived for eighty-one years, including forty-eight years after the shoot-out that day.

Either by marriage or by choice, Wyatt Earp made a somewhat, to me, more courageous decision to link most of his life and fate to the Jews. The Jews could have used a few more good men, like Wyatt Earp, in the dark years following his death. Men who didn't take forever to figure out who the bad guys were.

By chance, Wyatt Earp and my great-grandfather, Osher, lived almost exactly the same lifetime. Earp was born in 1848 in Illinois and died in Los Angeles in 1929, at eighty-one. Osher Katzman was born in 1852 in Byelorussia and died in Chicago in 1935, at eighty-three. He was the father of Jacob, who was my grandfather. This is where my grandparents came from and when they lived.

My father Irving's Parents:

Jacob Katzman, 1882 to 1961, born in Mogilev, Byelorussia, and came to America in 1901. He was a carpenter and worked on a Polish railroad before escaping across the Polish border by hiding under large mounds of hay in a hay wagon. He once told me, as I was sitting on his knee, that the border guards stuck rifles with long, sharp bayonets repeatedly into the hay to find any people trying to slip past them. But they just barely missed him as he flattened his skinny body against the rough wooden walls of the wagon. He later worked in Chicago as a carpenter in buildings along South Lake

Wyatt Earp
1848 - 1929

Osher Katzman
1852 - 1935

Shore Drive.

My father told me stories about how Jacob came home, bloodied from fights in his union hall when the first unions were being created. He was a socialist and believed all religion was just *bunk*. He was sawing wood in Windsor, Ontario when his heart gave out. I inherited all his tools and became quite accomplished as a carpenter, myself. He was the first and youngest of my four grandparents to die, at seventy-eight, when I was eleven.

Rose and Jacob Katzman on their wedding day in 1903

My grandfather, Jacob Katzman, seated far right, with his brothers, from the left: Wolf, Nathan, Norman, unknown, and David. Some people think I look just like my Uncle Norman. I do, too.

My Great-uncle Wolf Katzman, who came to American in 1902, joined the U.S. Army and fought against my Great-uncle Arnold Baumwohl, who was in the Hapsburg Emperor's army, in 1917 in World War I.

Rose Katzman, 1886 to 1979, born Epstein, in Vilna, Lithuania, then orphaned and adopted by relatives named Galin. She came to Newport, Kentucky in 1902 and married my grandfather, Jacob, in 1906. She raised five children, was a housewife and died at the age of ninety-three. I once wrote a poem to her about her wonderfully flavorful homemade tomato-rice soup. Rose was the second of my grandparents to die, when I was twenty-nine.

Jacob and Rose Katzman in 1960

My mother Anne's Parents:

Nathan Warman, 1893 to 1987, born in Minsk, Byelorussia, was on a boat halfway to America in 1914 when World War I broke out in the Austrian-Hungarian Empire. In 1913 he shaved a year off his age to escape serving in Czar Nicholas' army. Forty-five years later, he had to wait an extra year to collect social security, at sixty-six.

He was a businessman and also built houses. He had a vast Lionel Train set in his basement that I could look at, but not touch. The special love of his life was a lemon tree that he raised from a small twig in a pot, to a huge tree that filled most of his family room. It produced lemons the size of softballs. It was his baby and I remember how he cried when he had to leave it behind after he sold his home to move into a senior apartment complex. He lived to be ninety-four. He was my third grandparent to die, on the 4th of July, when I was thirty-seven.

Nathan Warman
1893 - 1987

Celia Warman, 1901 to 1997, born a Baumwohl, Turkingkopf on her mother's side, in Dobra, Poland. She raised three children and was also a businesswoman, running a cramped women's brassiere and girdle store in South-East Chicago, even before she learned to speak English. She vividly showed me how she used a kind of sign language to sell to women that she was unable to actually speak to, or even understand. She described how my then infant mother, Anne, and her brother, Milton, born eighteen months apart, slept in the bottom two drawers of an old dresser lined with soft blankets, in the back of her shop, while she worked in the front.

Celia came to America in 1918, at age seventeen and met Nathan who worked for her brother, Louis, in Whiting, Indiana. They went to night school together to learn English. After just one class, Celia decided that was enough of that, and then she married my grandfather. She lived for ninety-six years, and died when I was forty-seven. Celia was the last of my grandparents to die, and she wouldn't have had it any other way.

Celia Baumwohl Warman
1901–1997

If my grandmother, Celia Warman, had been with the Clanton Gang at the OK Corral in 1881, and had Wyatt Earp known that she was there with them, he would have wisely done some other thing that historic October day. Maybe play faro at his saloon in Tombstone. Earp, at six-foot-one, would have been no match for my four-foot-eleven inch Grandma, and he'd have known it, too.

Celia was twenty-eight when Wyatt Earp died, and she was a real beauty.

Petite, with large, dark-brown eyes, long, thick, dark-brown hair, an olive-colored complexion and a voluptuous figure, my Grandma told me that people in America thought she was a Gypsy.

Grandma faced down a man with a shotgun, who broke into her house when she was in her sixties. But unlike Wyatt Earp, she was unarmed. Except with a razor-sharp tongue and an intimidating fierceness in her dark eyes. She protected her younger sister, Shirley, and demanded that the invader allow her to get some pills for her heart, before she would talk to him. Only then, did she give him a small amount of money and told him that if he left her house immediately, she would not call the police, as if she held all the cards and was not his victim. That guy was lucky to get out of her house alive.

Young or old, when people met my Grandma Warman, they didn't soon forget her. She was the smartest, toughest person in my family.

When I was very young...too young...I first heard the story from my Grandma Warman about the devastating pogrom that came to her small village of Dobra, just outside of Krakow, Poland, in 1916.

A pogrom—a Russian word that means an organized massacre of a minority group, in this case, Jews—meant a hoard of Cossacks on huge horses would swoop down on a defenseless shtetl, or Jewish town, kill the men, rape the women and steal or kill the children. The anti-Semitic Austrian-Hungarian military authorities never interfered, and considered this a form of population control of a troublesome minority in their empire.

My grandmother, one of ten children, witnessed her grandfather, Moishe, being killed in one of these periodic attacks, in 1914. Two years later, while hiding with her mother, Fannie, behind the door of a large barn on the farm where her family raised cattle, Celia watched as her father dug a pit to bury some valuable family possessions, so no one would be able to steal them during the next pogrom.

There had been some warning from a friendly Polish-Catholic neighbor about what was coming, and her father, also named

Moishe, thought he'd have enough time to save some family treasures, before running off someplace to hide himself, as well. But as it turned out, there was no time. A Cossack suddenly appeared above him, while my great-grandfather was still digging the hole in the ground. The rampaging and pitiless Cossack raised his long, gleaming sword and swiftly beheaded my great-grandfather, letting his head roll into the freshly dug hole.

My Grandmother witnessed all of this from her hiding place. She told me the story several times. I believe she never recovered from the horrific experience. I noticed very early, in the mid-1950s, that whenever she smiled, or even laughed, the emotion never made it all the way up to her cold, dark eyes.

My Great-grandfather Moishe Baumwohl

She told me, also numerous times, that my middle name, Michael, was given to me in memory of her murdered father and grandfather.

Jews use the first letter of the name of a deceased relative that they wish to honor, when naming a newborn child. My parents wanted me to have an "American" sounding name to save me some grief down the road, so I was named (M)ichael instead of (M)oishe, in 1950.

But the name was drenched in blood when I was given it, and I couldn't separate my name from the story that came with it. The grief I was supposed to be avoiding by having an "American" sounding middle name may have worked on the strangers I met, but I was not spared the gruesome details when I first learned, at the age of five, "The Two Moishes Story."

Then I heard my Grandma's grim story about her older brother, Arnold.

Great-Uncle Arnold was in the Hapsburg Emperor's army, fighting against the United States, in 1917. That meant, ironically, that my mother's Uncle Arnold was in the enemy army fighting against my father's Uncle Wolf, who having arrived in America fifteen years earlier, was already in the United States Army.

My grandmother, Celia, left, standing behind her parents (my great-grandparents), Fannie and Moishe Baumwohl.

Uncle Arnold was in the cavalry, and was captured by the Russians after they defeated the Emperor's forces in some forgotten skirmish. He was then sent as a slave laborer to work in an elderly widow's small candy factory. He was the only worker there.

After a while, the lonely widow learned more about my Uncle and his young wife back in Poland, and she gradually took a liking to him. She told Uncle Arnold that she had no children of her own, and that if he were to send for his wife and new baby to come live in her little village, she would leave the factory to him at the war's end.

**My Great-uncle Arnold Baumwohl, a soldier in
World War I in 1917**

Uncle Arnold took the money the old widow offered him to buy train tickets and wired his wife the good news that she and their child should come to the little Russian village, right away.

Celia's mother, my Great-Grandmother Fannie, decided that Celia would be safer living in Russia than remaining in Poland. So she asked Celia to go to Russia with her new sister-in-law, as a helper with the baby, and also so Uncle Arnold's attractive young wife would not be traveling alone. They packed what little the two women could take with them and bought the train tickets to travel to Russia.

They were about to leave for the train station, when a cable arrived from the old Russian widow warning Uncle Arnold's wife not to come. The Russian Revolution had suddenly begun. Some local townspeople, living near the candy factory, mistakenly assumed that the young, male prisoner-of-war working in the factory was actually its Jewish, capitalistic owner. A mob of young men broke into the factory office early one morning and swiftly killed my Uncle Arnold.

My Great-grandmother Fannie Baumwohl

That made three deaths of Celia's very close family members in four years.

The two young women abandoned their original plans, split up, and my grandmother traveled west to Germany instead. She knew four different languages at that time (five, when she would learn English in the next few years): Polish, Ukraina, a regional dialect of Russian, could read Hebrew, and she spoke Yiddish every day.

Yiddish, is a Jewish language that had developed over a thousand years before, when Jews in large numbers began moving north and east into the area of Russia/Poland. It is a blend of mostly German, with Polish and Hebrew mixed into it. So my Grandmother was able to make herself understood while traveling north through Germany, to the seaport of Hamburg, alone. Her brother, Louis, already settled in Whiting, Indiana, had sent her money for a ticket on a ship to America, if she could somehow manage to get to Hamburg on her own.

My Grandma told me that she worked as a waitress in crowded German beer halls to pay her way across the country. This tiny, but quite strong woman had long ago proved this to her own doubting children by boldly barging into the kitchen of Chicago's famous German restaurant, Berghoff's. She was determined to show her children how she handled multiple beer orders from loud, impatient and boozy customers in Germany.

She lined up eight mugs of beer, to the astonishment of the kitchen staff, who were too intimidated to shoo her out of their kitchen. Then she balanced eight more mugs on top of the first eight. Then, grasping the handles of the four bottom mugs in each hand, my fearless Grandmother swept out of the restaurant's kitchen to show her speechless, and very embarrassed children, that she could indeed wait on sixteen customers at once, when she was a very sturdy teenager, as she had long claimed to them that she could still do. Satisfied that she had unequivocally proven her point, she returned the sixteen mugs to the still frozen kitchen staff and left Berghoff's Restaurant.

Colorful family stories aside, after those three terrible deaths of her grandfather, father and brother, the Grandmother I knew as a child in the early Fifties had just two emotions:

Angry and Angrier.

Receiving loving approval from my Grandma Warman was just not possible. Not for me, and not for my mother, Anne, who suffered

My teenaged grandmother, Celia Baumwohl (left), at fourteen in 1915, with her older brother Arnold's young wife, Sophia.

terrible emotional consequences because of it. It was as if the murderous Cossacks had followed all of us across the Atlantic Ocean, in their endless pursuit of defenseless Jews.

The damage resulting from the violent and unpreventable deaths of three of my ancestors in Central Europe continued to plague my mother's family and eventually me, in the Central United States, over fifty years after those events originally occurred.

1947 - Celia and Nathan Warman, seated left and right, with their children: Adele Warman, seated center, Milton Warman, standing left, with his wife, Shyrl, holding their new son, Ricky, and my parents, Anne Warman Katzman and Irving Katzman.

****

One day, in 1958, when I was eight, I asked my Grandma Warman what became of all her cousins, aunts and uncles who had remained in Poland after she emigrated to the United States, forty years before. It was a topic we had never discussed.

We were both in her warm and fragrant kitchen, where she always seemed to me to be cooking something wonderful. I was sitting at her kitchen table and she was standing by her double sink. The water was rushing from the faucet. Pots were bubbling on her gas stove. She suddenly stopped moving and slowly turned to look at me, her dark eyes...opaque. Her face was blank. I didn't comprehend the change in her manner at all. She seemed to be looking at something...far away...something...I couldn't see.

Then, in a lifeless voice, this normally dynamic woman said to me, to the walls,

"Hitler...took care of them."

With those potent words still hanging in the air, as if there were wooden clothespins holding the letters up, my Grandmother turned back to the sink, turned off the water, shut off the burners on the gas stove and abruptly left the kitchen, without another word. I did not understand what was happening or how my innocent question changed her behavior.

The name of Adolph Hitler never was spoken aloud by anyone in my family, as far back as I could remember. I knew nothing about the war in Europe. But I was a very curious child at eight, thirteen years after the end of World War Two. I was a fast reader, as well, retaining all I learned.

So, I began relentlessly reading everything I could find, to allow me to understand why my fierce Grandmother changed so dramatically, in response to a question I had never asked her before.

Dictionaries led me to Encyclopedias, and those led to children's history books about the War. That led me to my Hebrew School library to find out whatever had happened to the Jews in the war years. I was plunging into a spider-web of information that was too much, too soon, for me to know. But one fact led to another, and like an addict, unable to stop, I learned more, and more, and more.

Without comprehending the meaning of all the information pouring into my very young mind, I became voracious, seeking out adult history books in public libraries. I learned so many words I never knew before:

Holocaust...Star-of-David   yellow   patches...book-burning... selections...the Final Solution...extermination...

concentration camps...sterilization...the Warsaw Ghetto...
Dr. Mengele...Eichmann...Goering...Goebbels...
Himmler...Kristalnacht...   Cyclon-B gas *showers*...Juden
Frei!...Dachau...Treblinka...Auschwitz...Buchenwald...
Bergen-Belsen...many more such places of horror...and all
that poison from the adult world swirled and churned in
my brain.

USHMM Photo Archives

**Dutch Jews wearing prison uniforms marked with a
yellow star and the letter "N", for Netherlands, stand
at attention during a roll call at the Buchenwald
concentration camp (February 28, 1941).**

I read about experimentation on twins and pregnant women, all
forms of dehumanizing torture, degradation and all about the
seemingly invincible German army.

While my classmates played baseball and marbles on the school
playground, I drenched myself with a torrent of facts that I was not
yet able to stitch together, and really understand, as more than just
words on a page, numbly learning ever more, like I was memorizing
all the state capitols or multiplication tables. And all those words just
sat there...ticking...waiting for me to understand.

Then, in 1959, I saw the film: *The Diary of Anne Frank.*

What I thought was just one more war film, was so much more. It
was about a real family, trapped in an attic, hiding from the Germans

USHMM Photo Archives

Gen. Dwight Eisenhower and other U.S. Army officers view the bodies of executed prisoners while on a tour of the Obrdruf concentration camp (April 12, 1945).

in Holland. It was not about thousands of faceless soldiers shooting at each other, or battleships blowing each other out of the ocean. It was about a family of ordinary Jewish adults and children, laughing, bickering, and loving each other. I came to see their fear as a real thing and I began to experience it, like I was in that cramped attic, with them.

All through the movie, whenever the Germans would uncover ever more hiding Dutch Jews, there would come a kind of military paddy-wagon to round them up and take them away to the concentration camps. Whenever that wagon would appear, a very distinct siren would wail...softer then louder...softer then louder...as the wagon came closer and closer to capturing its trapped and doomed prey. This brassy siren sound was so very different than an American ambulance or police siren, that I was used to hearing. It was an alien sound to my nine-year-old ears.

The movie gradually became far more frightening than any make-believe monster movie, that I would see at some Saturday afternoon matinee.

As what I already knew, and what I now was seeing on the screen...slowly melded together...I began to understand. And then I became very afraid. Afraid for the Frank family, afraid for young Anne, and suddenly, for the first time...afraid for myself.

When the final scene of the movie unfolded, after the Jews in the attic are discovered by an informant to the Germans and that wailing sound begins and gets louder and louder and louder, screaming in my ears, and then I saw the German soldiers ripping away the false bookcase that hid the secret door to the attic where the Frank family waited, helplessly, I became overwhelmed with terror, and couldn't watch the last terrible moments on the screen.

Then, the nightmares began for me, and they lasted for years. I would hide under my covers, even in the summer before we had any air-conditioners, drenched in my sweat, hiding from the Germans, sure they would come for me, some night, any night, and nothing could stop them, and they would take me away to one of those concentration camps and start ripping apart my body. I would never be able to escape them.

This went on night after night. Even though I lived in a Jewish neighborhood, with friendly Irish neighbors, none of that could chase away the demons that pursued me in the dark of the night .

When enough time had passed, so that I could finally begin to sleep without nightmares, the understanding that I now possessed changed and became like a separate part of me, like a thing that lived within me. As the years passed and I became fifteen, twenty and thirty...the agony that the Jews had endured, along with millions of other kinds of people...settled deep inside of me. A combination of vulnerability, anger, rage and an uncomprehending mystification that God would let monsters do these things to us, became a kind of...howling in my soul...an unimaginable level of evil done on such a monumental scale to so many millions, that no fantasy of revenge could ever chase away the terrible reality that I had forced myself to learn.

I knew so much more than almost anyone I met about what had happened to the Jews, and I was...cursed by my quest. The grim results of my determination to understand my Grandmother's strange and indelible reaction to my simple question, when I was just eight years old, lasted almost forty years, and only began to subside with her death, at the age of ninety-six, in 1997.

I learned that a person did not have to actually experience the Holocaust firsthand to become another a victim of it, to be a prisoner of it, and that a terror trapped in one's mind is a very real terror, indeed.

Even today, I can still see and feel what my Grandmother must have felt, in 1958, and...oh, God...I so wish...I could take back my question to her.

For both of us.

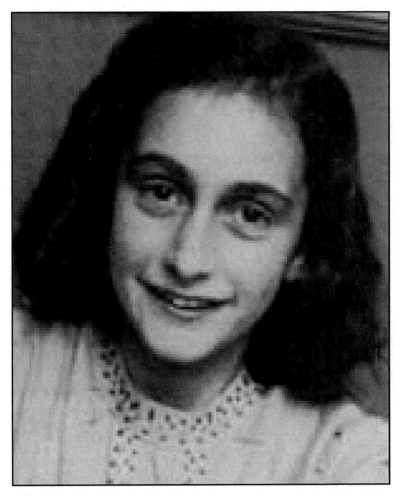

After being betrayed to the Nazis, Anne, her family and the others living with them were arrested and deported to Nazi concentration camps. In March of 1945, nine months after she was arrested, Anne Frank died of typhus at Bergen-Belsen. She was fifteen years old.

... ...And then, the nightmares began for me... ... ...

AUSCHWITZ...BERGEN-BELSEN...BUCHENWALD...*(8 years old)*
...CHELMO...DACHAU...*(8 years old)*...MAJDANIK...SERED...
(8 years old)...MAUTHAUSEN...PLASZOW...RAVENSBRUCK...
SACHSENHAUSEN...*(8 years old)*...SOBIBOR...THERESIENSTADT...
TREBLINKA...FINAL SOLUTION...KRYSTALNACHT...*(8 years old)*

HITLER...GOERING...HIMMLER
(8 years old)
DR. MENGELE...WARSAW GHETTO
(8 years old)
EXTERMINATION...STERILIZATION

NOW THEY ARE COMING FOR ME...

NOW THEY ARE COMING FOR ME...

NOW...
THEY ARE COMING FOR ME!!!

(8...YEARS...OLD)

and they lasted......

and lasted......

for years......

Although I am nearly fifty-six now, I have never been able to totally suppress my childhood fear that some...superhuman force...will rise up to snuff out the Jews. Even though I have never been in...or even near...a real concentration camp, I now realize, nevertheless, that a part of me will never be able to escape from the horror that happened there.

But I also know that the rest of me, filled with the undying spirit of my defiant and courageous Grandmother, Celia Warman, will **never** surrender to any such evil force.

I believe, to my core, that:
God put the Jews on this planet for a purpose.
His purpose.
And...**nothing!**
No one!
No power on earth!
Will **<u>ever</u>** destroy...the Jewish People.

Amen.

Infamous concentration camp entrance gate photo, in German lying that "Work will make you free."

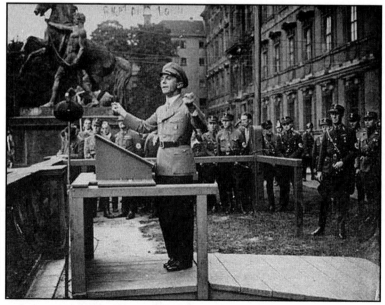

Propaganda Minister Joseph Goebbels delivers a speech at an SA gathering for the Hoerst Wessel brigade in the Berlin Lustgarten (August 25, 1935)

*In **my** world, you didn't sell out your friends.*

They were not a chip to be used in negotiations.

If a friend stuck his, or her, neck out to aid me, unasked, in a situation where I was clearly outgunned, I could not comprehend turning around and offering that friend up as a sacrifice to save my own skin.

Such a concept was beyond my comprehension.

The very asking of me to turn over a name was an insult, to me.

Had they no sense of the impossibility of what they wanted?

6

A Short Story without a Name

Note: To the gentlemen and ladies of the jury, and all principled lawyers, everywhere. While the heart and soul of the following story is totally true, my being an alert Jewish boy and not some naïve legal imbecile, demands that I declare these words:

*I want to make it very clear that certain specific facts concerning ages and physical descriptions of some of the characters in my story have been altered in order to disguise their true identities. Not even **one** of them, is actually a spawn of the Devil.*

*Also, my descriptions of the opposing attorneys' lush office and some other details have been creatively modified for the same reasons. The only statement that I will fearlessly attest to being unequivocally true, is that like in all high-powered law offices everywhere, the secretaries were **very, very** pretty.*

So then, except for these disclaimers, consider me to be still under oath, sort of...

So, what is the nature of friendship?
Here is one view that may help define it.

In 1978, I was embroiled in a contentious lawsuit with another distribution company in the Chicago area. They were, for a very long time, the only game in town, and I sought to enter their market and compete with them.

This notion displeased them.

In the ensuing battle between us for their existing accounts, they resisted as any company with a lock on a market might, but I felt their manner of attempting to retain their virtual one hundred per cent market share to be unreasonable, as did some of the customers that wanted to switch suppliers.

I asked my lawyer if there was any recourse to what I felt was unfair competition, and he sent me to an associate of his that did that sort of litigation.

The man my lawyer sent me to was very formal, but friendly, almost courtly in his manner. I was twenty-eight at the time, and I believe he was about fifty. He had a slight southern accent and after a

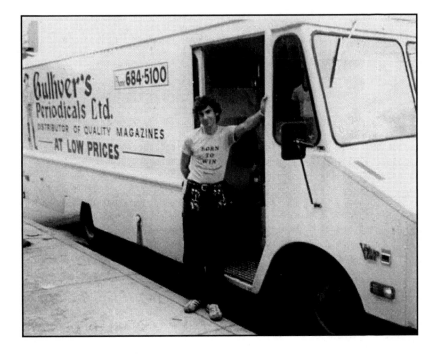

while, I was to learn, a very subtle sense of humor.

He listened patiently, courteously, to my description of the other company's tactics that I felt were intimidating to their captive market, and periodically asked me to clarify this point or that. His manner was very calm, and unemotional.

He decided, after considering all the information that I had given him, that if in fact all that I said was true, that the other company was engaging in unreasonable restraint of trade under the Robinson-Patman Act.

He agreed to represent me with no fee with the understanding that if we prevailed in our suit, that his firm would receive a percentage of the monetary damages award.

After he notified the other company of his intentions to discover if there was, in fact, any evidence of my assertions about their behavior in my battle to enter their market, they referred him to their own law firm located in the top floors of this architecturally distinctive and imposing building in downtown Chicago.

He agreed to represent me with no fee with the understanding that if we prevailed in our suit, that his firm would receive a percentage of the monetary damages award.

After he notified the other company of his intentions to discover if there was, in fact, any evidence of my assertions about their behavior in my battle to enter their market, they referred him to their own law firm located in the top floors of this architecturally distinctive and imposing building in downtown Chicago.

When I learned the name of the other law firm, it did give me some pause. I was involved in a divorce proceeding at that particular time, and they were the same people who were representing my wife.

After my initial apprehensive reaction to this very unsettling news, I decided that in view of the overwhelming odds against me in my competitive struggle, and the size of the legal muscle representing my then wife, that if I was going to go to hell, I may as well go *all* the way to hell, and just accepted the news with resignation.

After some back and forth communication between my lawyer and theirs, a date was set to begin the "discovery process". This is a procedure where each side is allowed to interrogate the other, so as to learn all the necessary facts that each side will present in court to make their case. That way, each side will have time to adequately provide a defense, if possible, and eliminate the chance that one side will produce a "surprise" in court that the other side isn't prepared for.

This is a long established legal practice that benefits all sides, and we began what was to be a very long dreary process of endless questions spread over many weeks.

During this period, my lawyer coached me on how to answer so as to not make this process any longer than necessary, and I listened intently to all that he said. After all, he was making no money per hour, and he was all I had to defend me from the giant that I was opposing.

When we first exited the elevator after a very long ride up into the clouds, it seemed to me, and entered the lair of our enemy's forces, I was really surprised by how large a company it was. We stopped at the receptionist's desk to ask where we were supposed to go, and she pointed down a long corridor, and we followed her finger down to the conference room to meet the other side's attorney.

When we opened the door, we were greeted by a *mob* of lawyers!

There were at least a dozen men sitting there, or more, seated on three sides of a very long table. They represented not only the local company that we were suing, but also, all the national magazine distribution companies that refused to supply me directly.

When my lawyer first informed me that we would be going to the other side's office for the questioning, I was offended and indignantly asked him why those guys didn't have to come to us. My lawyer gently soothed my wounded ego with his calm manner and soft words, saying, that if we went to their office and didn't like how we were treated, we could always get up...and leave.

He was trying to get it across to me that going to them did not make us supplicants—that we still had power of our own. I was newly educated, and mollified.

Their very long interview of me included questions about my life, my company, what I read, who I had spoken to about my case, how I ran my business, the history of my business, what proof I had of my assertions about their client's practices and even, to my surprise, what was the English translation of the Hebrew words I had written on the front of my truck.

While I will decline to repeat that translation this many years later, I will say that it brought a gasp and a burst of laughter from most of the lawyers on the opposing side, even though it was quite aggressively uncomplimentary to their own client.

That same group of Hebrew letters frequently caught the eye of men that appeared to me to be Orthodox or Hasidic Jews, by their manner of dress. I was always amused as they stopped suddenly as they were passing the front of my white truck, while I was sitting at a red light.

These men would back up, read the letters and try to make sense of them, while examining my face through the windshield to see who would write such a thing on the front of his truck. Then they would go on their way, shaking their heads in confusion.

What they didn't know, was that the words were really English, but written in Hebrew letters. They couldn't be translated by a Hebrew speaker, because they had no meaning in that language.

It was admittedly a funny moment, the only one, in a very serious lawsuit, with a lot of money riding on the outcome. No matter what happened, the lawyers defending my opponent had to be costing them a fortune.

While this was all happening, a letter came to my newsstand one day, with no return address.

Inside was a memo to the appropriate persons in the other company's various departments, on the company's letterhead, telling them to follow a course of action in regards to my competition, that would seal our case against them.

There was another, smaller handwritten note to me that said simply, "Bob, I thought this might be helpful to you." It was signed by a longtime friend of mine, who worked for that company, at that time.

Before I became their competition, I had been one of the larger company's largest independent accounts. For almost ten years, I was at their distribution center every week, knew everybody, was friendly with everyone from the guys who operated the forklifts to the frequently very pretty customer service girls. I knew many of their truck drivers and the men who delivered the magazine racks. I knew the president of the company, the owner, who was a different person, and the various executives who ran different departments.

There were a lot of older Jewish guys working there that regarded me as a young, also Jewish go-getter that perhaps reminded themselves of their own youth. We had an easy, though always respectful on my end, camaraderie.

I was popular there, sold a ton of magazines, and it was a really nice customer/supplier relationship.

In other words, there were hundreds of employees there who I knew, some of whom had a lot of empathy for my struggle against their own employer, and anyone of them could have surreptitiously removed that incriminating letter from the office and sent it to me.

It may also have happened because among the hundreds of really nice people working at that huge company, there were about three that I ended up butting heads with over some significant issues, and that gave birth to my desire to compete with them.

These persons were not universally adored at that company, so that may also have prompted the secret attempt to aid me.

While all of the above is, or could be, true, in actuality, the note was sent from someone whom I was friendly with outside of the company as well, who had been to my house, had bobbed for apples with my child on Halloween, and was someone for whom I had great respect and affection.

So I knew well who the sender of the valuable document was.

The next day, I gave the letter to my lawyer, without the note from my friend.

He was quite surprised, and pleased as this was the first material piece of evidence that proved our case.

When he asked me how I obtained the item, I murmured that it was sent to me from an old friend who was an employee of the company we were opposing, but I said no more than that.

My lawyer, who by then was someone I was becoming friendlier with, as he got to know me and gained an appreciation of the impossibility of my desire to compete with this giant firm, regarded the letter with silent amazement, and then studied me for a long moment. But he said no more about it, and I went back to my struggle on the streets below his office.

He sent the letter by messenger to the other law firm, and we both waited for the explosion.

It was not long in coming.

The lead consul for the other company's law firm called my lawyer in a rage that a private communication intended only for use as an inter-office memo should find its way into hostile hands. He demanded that we appear before his team of lawyers to answer for this intolerable outrage to his client.

We showed up the next day.

Their lead consul was a large middle-aged man of no humor and smoldering contempt for us that he made no effort to disguise. His voice conveyed his boredom with this whole enterprise and suggested that we were not worth his time. While several of the other attorneys were cordial—a little joshing back and forth with my lawyer before each session started, or during the coffee breaks—the lead guy remained cold and distant, speaking only to us when the clock started and his meter was running.

I guess he didn't feel like kidding around now, either, since we had a knife pressed against his client's throat, so to speak.

He thundered at my attorney about this completely unethical behavior, and was this the manner in which we were going to conduct ourselves in this lawsuit?

My lawyer didn't exactly yawn during the other guy's tirade, but he didn't recoil, either. He just sat quietly while the previously disinterested lead consul, who now displayed a newfound energy and devotion to his client, concluded his umbrage.

Then the man turned to me, and in a stern and steely voice demanded that I tell him, right now, who was the source of the letter.

I looked at this creature in disbelief, as if he had just grown antlers, and I said to him:

"No."

He then looked at me as if I were some disgusting kind of fungus and demanded, once again, that I immediately disgorge my source.

With no hesitation at all, I just said, again, but more insistently,

"No!"

I thought the other man was going to have heart failure from his complexion's rapidly deepening color from pink to red to purple.

He turned to my attorney to inquire if he was unaware of the rules of discovery, as if he were speaking to a very small boy, and that he (my attorney) must compel me to provide them with a name, or face serious consequences. Then he turned his back on us and left the conference room, letting the door close with a bang of expensive wood hitting expensive wood.

There was a silence in the room for a bit.

My lawyer and I had not discussed how I should respond to this particular blunt question. We just showed up in response to their summons to see, I guess, their reaction to our evidence.

As I had been a heretofore quite respectful and cooperative client, following all of my lawyer's instructions, it possibly had not occurred to him that I would exhibit resistance to established legal norms.

But I had not anticipated that there would be a challenge to *my* quite firmly established rules of behavior.

In *my* world, you didn't sell out your friends.

They were not a chip to be used in negotiations.

If a friend stuck his, or her, neck out to aid me, unasked, in a situation where I was clearly outgunned, I could not comprehend turning around and offering that friend up as a sacrifice to save my own skin.

Such a concept was beyond my comprehension.

The very asking of me to turn over a name was an insult.

Had they no sense of the impossibility of what they wanted?

My lawyer broke the silence and told me that I would have to give them a name.

I sat for a moment trying to sort this out. My guy expected that I would do for him what I wouldn't do for anyone? He needed to understand that I meant what I said.

That it wasn't just for show.

I turned to him and quietly explained that if I revealed the identity of my friend, that person would be fired, lose all his/her benefits and profit sharing, and throw his/her family into economic turmoil. This was not how I repaid the kindness of a friend.

He needed to know that I didn't pay someone to sneak into the company's offices late one night to ransack their files and steal damaging private memos. That all the initiative was on the other side, and that I felt no guilt, or compulsion to rat out my friend, to satisfy what I felt was some immoral legal requirement.

My lawyer responded that there could be consequences to me, and to him if I refused the request to provide a name.

I couldn't believe that this very decent man was unable to see that there existed codes of behavior that were unbreakable. That in my world a person who would sell out another to save themselves was completely contemptible and undeserving of true friends.

That having a real friend was one of the rarest treasures in a man's life, far too valuable to offer up as a defense at the first sign of peril.

I said these things to my lawyer out loud then, to help him see that I really had no choice. A man had honor, or he did not.

A man was worthy of the trust of a friend, or he was not.

But what I did *not* tell my lawyer was that this friend and I had had a serious argument some months prior to this day, and that we hadn't spoken in all that time in between. That my friend's choosing to help me in my time of clear need transcended the unresolved issues between us, and made me all the more wondrous about how much our older relationship was treasured.

That our private troubles were ours alone, and that my friend would not abandon me to danger from others, and trusted, unasked, that my values were the same, and that there would be no risk to my friend by his/her choosing to do what he did. Or she did.

My attorney studied me while I laid out my beliefs to him. He did not interrupt me, and listened with absorption as I explained that consequences to me would in no way alter my behavior.

He said nothing in response, but I am sure that I saw the tiniest twinkle in his eye, as if the mischief my position would cause would be worth the risk.

He lowered his head with a very small smile, as if to consider what to do. Then deciding, he rose, went to the door and asked the lovely secretary in the next room to tell the other attorneys to return to the conference room, that we were ready to respond.

When all the men filed back in and took their seats around their side of the table, my lawyer stood and said, firmly, that his client, me, would absolutely not supply them with the name of the sender of the memo. That his client felt his friend would be at significant risk, and that there would be no compromise on this matter, period.

The lead consul for the other side looked at us as if we were brain-damaged and stated, angrily, that the name would be held in strict confidence and, damn it, didn't we trust them?

My attorney responded, in a clear voice,

"No."

I loved him for it.

He said that part on his own.

While the lead consul stared at us both in disbelief, I noticed as I looked around the room that one after another of the younger attorneys began to smile, some covering their mouths with their hands, as if it was uncontrollably contagious, until someone laughed out loud at the very idea that a man would so boldly speak the truth, in this room *filled* with lawyers.

The laughter spread with a ripple around their side of the table until we, too, smiled at the unlikeliness of this response to our determined resistance to their demand.

Everyone smiled except the very serious lead consul, who I guess knew when the tide had turned against him, who maybe even saw that there could indeed be honor among men, and he sighed an audible sigh of what I would like to think of as his acceptance of an "insignificant defeat," and he turned to his amused colleagues, and said,

"Let's move on."

The attorney's demand, and that fundamental issue…were never raised again.

All through the next two nights, I struggled with my strangely uncharacteristic willingness to surrender something so valuable to me.

Although there was so much I could do nothing about, the Castle took on a symbolic meaning to me that transcended practicality, and if I could summon a little imagination, and some gumption, this frustrating story might have a different ending.

Just because the moment with a huge and mysterious St. Bernard, five months earlier, had taken on a fairytale quality that now seemed silly to me as time passed, my wooden Castle was very real and part of my family's history. Why let it go?

The black night sky slowly gave birth to a new day's glow.

7

The Foreclosure Quintet

Part I:
...and Along Came this Dog...

January 7, 2006—Elvis Presley's seventieth birthday.

How ever the rest of America celebrated the King of Rock 'n Roll's big day, I spent it making perhaps my thirtieth trip, steadily moving out of my beloved old house.

My fertile half-acre in affluent Highland Park, Illinois, turned out to be too expensive a place to keep in light of my declining fortunes. Doctor/Lawyer/Dot.Com Land was no longer a safe environment for a guy like me that sold old magazines and newspapers for a living, *when* I could still sell them. The next generation was glued to buying whatever they wanted from a computer screen, so my history-filled store that went back three hundred years, was no longer a Mecca for gift givers.

Because I shunned the internet and e-Bay as too remote and too cold a way for me to do business, many people thought that *I* was the actual antique who was still trying to sell antique paper by talking to real live people.

Three months after listing our house with a local broker, not one person had made a bid for our modest home, as the selling price steadily dropped ever lower. The dozen lovely and delicate River Birches and the seven broad and leafy Norway Maples that my wife and I planted and nurtured were not enticing enough to slow down the busy, busy people in our area to gaze on the beauty we had created over the years.

So, to save the cost of a professional mover, my wife and companion of thirty years, Joyce, my daughter, Sarah, aged nine, and I began moving out our lifetime jumble of things before the ax fell from our salivating mortgage company, who was patiently waiting to grab our house.

We had found a nice little place, a smaller house with far less land, a few miles away. Every morning and every night, the three of us filled up and emptied out our big old 1990 Chevy Van. We did this seven days a week, transferring what seemed to be an ocean of boxes

going to a too small island, and wondering how all this misery would turn out.

So on this glum Saturday morning, as I trudged up and down the stairs carrying ever more boxes and whatever else I could get my arms around, my mind was filled with the distant sound of laughter and squeals from my four children echoing through the now empty rooms. Three of them, Lisa Heather, David Jacob and Rachel Jennifer, had grown up and moved away, but their younger selves still ran rampant and carefree across our beautiful land, in my reveries.

I still saw ghostly crowds of friends and relatives gathering to celebrate birthdays, anniversaries, graduations, Thanksgiving Day and all the Jewish holidays.

I still saw both of my aged parents, hearing their weakening voices from when each of them lived with us just before they died, a year apart.

I still saw the last three of us living there, out of the original nine, snuggling together on a soft old couch in a blackened room watching a magical fire crackling and hissing as it hungrily gobbled up log after log to fill its bottomless stomach.

I remembered us all sleeping together under soft quilts as that raging fire melted down to a molten black and orange pulsating glow, flickering all through the night.

All of this was playing like an endlessly repeating old home movie as I was robotically making the many trips up and down the stairway in my silent home, working alone that particular morning.

But then, as I was turning a corner from a second floor bedroom to descend the stairs, from the top step I saw…a giant white dog… on the bottom step, looking up at me.

I froze.

A massive expanse of white with splashes of orange, brown and black, it was a panting St. Bernard. Its gaping jaws hung open showing its black gums and many teeth. Its drooping, sad, wet eyes kept looking up at me, and didn't blink. So we looked at each other, in the silence. He seemed to me to be the size of a Volkswagen, with hair.

With my aching arms filled with heavy wooden dresser drawers, I cautiously, slowly, continued down the stairs, through the living room toward my open kitchen door, fifty feet away.

That big snowman of a dog followed me every step of the way into the kitchen, where I quietly set down the wooden drawers on a counter top and slowly shut the kitchen door, with the two of us both still inside. I pushed the door until I heard the latch click.

Where We Lived, Once Upon A Time...

What follows is a series of pictures of the many members of my family, which includes the Katzmans, Bishops, Warmans, Coles, Wisters and also many friends from my thirty years together with my wife, Joyce.

The pictures are not identified individually like a police line-up. Rather, they are meant to convey all the vitality that filled the walls of our lovely home. The people were there because we wanted them there to celebrate all the good things, like anniversaries, birthdays, graduations and for no reason at all.

Joy and I decided to try and buy the home after our youngest daughter, Sarah, came into our lives in 1996. It took a while, and a lot of cooperation from people who cared about us to buy that home, but we finally bought it in 1997, dreaming it would be our last home ever.

Fate decreed otherwise.

Since Sarah was the driving motivation to buy that home to start with, her picture opens this portfolio, and it ends it, too...with Sarah's lovely laughing face. I prefer to remember our house that way. Filled with laughter, which it was, and not silent and empty, as it is now.

Trick or Treat

Getting Together...

Family

Cousins

Happy Birthday, Sarah!

An Aunt Adele hug!

Family

Family

Family

Family

Loved ones

Precious

This is where I first saw the giant dog when I began walking down the stairs.

I kept going up and down the stairs carrying boxes, filling up the kitchen. The dog kept following me, his tongue hanging out, panting from climbing all those stairs. Seeing this, I started rooting around under the kitchen sink and found a large, clean, plastic bowl. I filled it to the top with cold tap water and set it on the floor in front of the dog, splashing my fingers in it, so he got the idea that the water was for him.

The dog stood there immobile and kept watching me.

So I picked up the bowl, held it closer to the dog's big muzzle, splashed a little water on his face, and then set it back down on the floor in front of him. Finally, thirsty, but still suspicious of me, the dog lowered its huge mouth to the bowl and began noisily lapping up the water, its ham-like tongue scattering small puddles on the floor.

Backing away from the dog, I grabbed a phone and called the Highland Park cops, whispering into the phone while the dog was still drinking, and told them to get over to my house--right away--and pick up the lost dog. They told me no one had reported a missing dog. Hanging up, I wondered how it was that the dog's owners didn't notice that their pet animal, *the size of a small dinosaur*, was missing.

Facing page: This is what the dog saw when he looked up the stairs at me.

This is the kitchen door where the giant dog entered my old house. I slammed it shut to trap him inside until the police came to get him. Later, I ran out this same door with the giant dog bounding after me.

Saint Bernard

My initial impression upon meeting the St. Bernard.

Returning to the still slurping dog, letting it see and smell my hands, I slowly put my arms around its neck, feeling for a collar with a dog tag on it, but there was none. The big dog let me do this, perhaps thinking I was hugging him. I let him think that.

After about five minutes, I saw an odd-looking Highland Park Police vehicle pull into my driveway. I noticed that it had an electric lift-gate attached to the back of it, as I observed it through my kitchen window.

The driver, a tall thin cop, walked past the now closed kitchen entrance over to my front door. I let the man in, and although he was initially quiet and serious, the cop warmed up when I showed him the watchful St. Bernard, who came over to quietly examine the cop. Then I got out of the way to see what the cop would do.

He attempted to put a wide strong red fabric leash around the huge dog's neck, but the irritated dog kept shaking it off. The cop kept trying, and failing. He seemed exasperated.

I asked the cop if I could help him, since the dog and I already knew each other. He agreed, skeptically.

Approaching the dog from the front, I began scratching behind both of its floppy ears, at the same time looking into his eyes, and then letting my hands drop down either side of its face, scratching his fur as I went. I made long, smooth strokes on both sides of the dog's face, from its ears to its neck, calming him, caressing him.

The dog lifted its eyes to look at me, and then raised its nose into the air, enjoying the attention and the doggy massage. I had learned as a child in the mid-Fifties how to relax a dog—all kinds of dogs—by doing that to them.

Dogs *like* me...always have. They trust me. I don't project menace, and I believe that a dog can sense kindness in a person, as well as evil.

People often say that when they think a dog is *really* smart...that the dog is *almost human*. Well, frankly, *I* think, when a dog *really* likes me, trusts me, then the *dog's* highest compliment is that he thinks that...*I'm almost a dog*. One of *them*.

I'd consider that high praise, if it were true. People are not necessarily more important than dogs, in the grand scheme of things.

As I kept stroking the dog, who kept its nose pointed up to the ceiling to better enjoy the massage, the cop who had been watching all of this, figured out what I was doing and quickly slipped the red leash over the dog's muzzle and ears, and pulled it up tight.

The surprised animal looked at me, with its wounded wet eyes, but I kept stroking his face, hoping he would forgive me. I felt weirdly guilty.

When the cop tried to drag the now docile dog out of the same front door where the cop first entered my house—our beautiful, wooden front door that my wife and I had custom-made, years before, with its beveled glass that made little rainbows all over our floor and walls when the sun shone through it, that now we were leaving behind us—the dog refused to go with him. He put his big floppy paws stiffly in front of himself and simply refused to budge. He looked up at the cop with defiance, as if to say,

"What're ya gonna do now, huh? *Carry me?*"

The cop tugged the leash, not meanly, but the stubborn dog would simply not walk out the wide open front door. As I watched this odd scene, I called out to the weary cop,

"Hey, follow me, Officer…the dog wants to go out the same way he came in. He doesn't trust the door *you* came in. He doesn't know it. C'mon, follow me!"

"Hey, Dog!" I yelled to the St. Bernard. He turned to look at me, his Benedict Arnold. The dog saw me run past him and he immediately galloped after me, dragging the startled cop behind him, right out the kitchen door, without a pause.

There was another cop out there, waiting, leaning on a squad car. He had the hard, tough face of an old boxer. But when he saw the big snowball of a dog come barreling after me out of the kitchen door, the cop's granite face split into a wide grin. It made him look almost handsome.

Waiting outside with the second cop was what appeared to me to be an Hispanic couple standing next to a big, black, shiny SUV. They were clearly overjoyed to find what must have been their lost pet, since the dog ran right over to them and danced around, happily. The cop with the leash had long ago given up any hope of controlling the situation…or the dog.

It was such an unexpected, spontaneously happy scene, so different from the forlorn emptiness that filled me as I was removing my last possessions from the silent house. Here were all these strangers, gathered together in my driveway—where no one else would ever gather again to come to see my family because of a birthday or some other special occasion.

All because of a lost dog.

I had this surreal flash that maybe the dog had lived here in some past life, or some fantasy like that, and then seeing the open door to his former home, the dog came bounding inside for a last look around.

Shaking off that strange thought, I approached the Hispanic couple and shook hands with the man, who looked to be in his forties, as did his wife. I had heard them speaking rapid Spanish so, dredging up my shaky high school vocabulary, I ventured,

"Um…como se llama…ah…su perro?" quietly assuming to myself that the enormous dog's name was "Hulk" or something epic like that.

But the smiling husband turned to me and replied, "Rocky."

I smiled back at him, and thought to myself, "Of course."

Above, the view from the kitchen door of my driveway where the police were waiting in their strange vehicle, and Rocky's owners in their shiny new SUV.

Below, the same view of the driveway looking toward my old house from the street.

I knelt by the cheery dog who stopped his dancing around and turned his huge shaggy face toward me with his big wet tongue hanging out, saliva dripping off of it, his happy-sad droopy eyes boring into me, and I gave him a big hug—a *real* hug this time—and said goodbye to him.

In seconds, all of the people parked in my driveway dispersed in three directions as we all went our separate ways, after *"muchas gracias"* and *"adios"* was repeatedly said by the happy couple to the cops and more intensely, to me.

In my case, after stopping at my local post office, I went to a McDonalds about two miles south of my house for a quick bite before racing to open up my old back-issue magazine store to catch the Saturday morning traffic. It was perhaps twenty minutes since I pulled out of my driveway.

When I entered the McDonalds, there was only one man in line ahead of me. It was that tall cop who first came for Rocky in response to my call to the Police. He turned and noticed me as I walked in the door and we both smiled at the oddness of the moment of our meeting again, for the second time, so soon. But neither of us said anything about it.

As he was waiting for his order, I decided to ask him,

"So, what's that big electric lift-gate on the back of your van used for?"

The cop quietly replied,

"Well, sometimes...we have to pick up dead deer off the highway..." and he made a face that told me he didn't enjoy doing that. I nodded my understanding and then said to him,

"Y'know, Officer, I go to sleep at night with my Beagle's muzzle resting on my left shoulder, snuggling next to me. Betsy, the Beagle."

The cop smiled at this cozy image and murmured,

"Yeah, I'm a dog lover, too..." and then walked off to a table on the other side of the restaurant to join his partner.

I raced out of the Golden Arches with my hot little bag of food, soon to be devoured on the way to my store and then I turned on the radio, already tuned to a hip new oldies station. As I drove my old red van toward the interstate with yet another load of stuff to cram into that smaller house, I had a smile on my face. There hadn't been a smile there for quite a while.

Then a thought flickered across my mind, just for a second, like a revelation:

Maybe Rocky wasn't just a dog, after all.

Maybe, he was...*hope*...coming to see me.

Hope, hidden behind sad, droopy eyes and a big black wet nose.

Maybe, just maybe, things would work out for the best, after all.

Maybe, instead of moving away from something I felt I'd lost...I was really moving closer to something else...something...*good*.

Just then, the radio announcer said, in his deep announcer's voice:

"And the number one song on January 7, 1956 was..."

and Elvis Presley's husky young voice rocked the air in my car, as he sang,

"You ain't nothin' but a hound dog,
Crockin' all the time..."

I laughed out loud at the radio and that wonderful song and yelled out,

"Perfect, Elvis! That's just perfect!"

Part II

Not Necessarily...

Part III:
Abandoning My Children's Castle:
A Dragon Evicted

Some thoughts on losing a piece of my life:

On June 22, 2006, I received an official letter from the 19th Judicial Circuit Court informing me that the modest brick and frame home my wife Joy and I lovingly began remodeling, planted twenty-two trees on the land, celebrated nearly one hundred birthdays, anniversaries, Chanukahs, Passovers, Rosh Hashanas, New Years, Thanksgivings, graduations, and watched countless fires flicker, hiss and crackle through the frigid Midwestern winter nights...was sold to the highest bidder by my mortgage company to some real estate investment corporation for $445,500.

We received not a penny from the sale.

We also expect that after all the "i's" were dotted and the "t's" were crossed, strong men driving bulldozers and machines with heavy steel wrecking balls would rumble up the sides of the gently sloping hill that our house rested upon, crushing the endless perennial flowers and China rose bushes my wife planted, and level the old place within a few days.

The ghostly molecules of thousands of childish giggles, laughs, tears and the ecstatic barks of all of our dogs, happy that someone they loved had finally come home to pet them and walk them, will finally escape the walls that heard them and contained them in one final wheeze of dust, as the plaster and timbers of those walls collapse and crumble and those long ago ordinary, yet precious, sounds of our lives rise in an invisible swirl as they join the winds blowing across our lost land, and disperse into the universe.

****

We had moved out the previous November, beginning the day after celebrating our last Thanksgiving Dinner there with many old friends, to a much smaller rented house a few miles away. Squeezing six bedrooms down to four required shedding possessions. Choices had to be made. What exactly is indispensable?

Using my own van over a period of seven months, I had completely emptied the house of furniture, toys, books, clothing, garden and hand tools, pictures, dishes, pots, pans, food, rugs, candles, flashlights and a refrigerator full of food. A pantry full of all the stuff that fills up a kitchen. So many little plastic containers and gadgets that you never realize you own. They must have seemed to be a good idea, once upon a time.

But we also shed much furniture, light fixtures, clothing, way too many books, old toys our grown-up kids no longer treasured...but then they changed their minds and came running back to grab that favorite stuffed animal they simply couldn't sleep without, twenty years ago. Now those long forgotten treasures will sit in the dark corners of *their* closets until they move somewhere else, someday.

Our synagogue and also a certain Catholic church we had old connections to, once upon a time, became the beneficiaries of truckloads of things we couldn't take with us. Clothing from my dead parents that I felt I had to hold onto. No more. Bits and pieces of our previous lives were scattered all around the great Metropolis.

Joy and I dug up and transplanted as many flowers as we could save, an endless number of flagstones and hundreds of bricks to create some new flower beds and also widen the small driveway of our new home. My old cranky lower back and I agreed to take smaller loads and make many more trips, but I had no choice in the matter. Too many bricks at one time was all it would take to put me out of commission for weeks. There is nothing macho about an out-of-whack, lower back. Smart older people learn to respect their body's limitations. There comes a time when you no longer have anything to prove to anyone else about your invincibility.

We took our cedar swing that I built myself, with its beautiful weathered grey patina, that used to sit between the two giant oaks outside our kitchen window. We would swing in it together on cool autumn nights with either a sleeping child or a curled up dog resting in our laps, or both, and silently listen to the clatter of dark parchment leaves blow in waves across our grass...dimly visible to us in the pale moonlight. In the frigid winters, the swing would sit and wait for us, mounds of crusty snow covering its arms, seat and shoulders, like a mute sentinel watching over our sleeping grass and flowers.

The last living thing to leave with us was a beautiful, graceful and delicate Japanese maple that I received as a Father's day gift in June 2002. I planted the petite tree with my own hands, watching over it,

The two 80 foot oak trees that snuggled our cedar swing. It was the focal point of our lovely yard, and identified our house in the neighborhood.

The Grannie Annie Memorial Garden

When my father, Irving, died in May 2000, I planted trees for him in Israel, just outside Jerusalem.

When my mother, Anne, died in 2001, such a gesture was no longer possible for me, financially, but creating an equivalent memorial for her in a Jewish manner was imperative to me.

So after much thought and much searching, Joy and I found a remarkable hi-bred tree called a Variegated Maple, or Harlequin maple. It was a beautiful, majestic tree.

We found them in a small Wisconsin nursery and planted three of them: my mother in the middle, a tree representing her younger sister, Adele, on her left and a third tree on her right representing her younger brother, Milton.

I felt one tree was too lonely and that my mother would be happier, in spirit, with a little company.

I sure hope no real estate developer cuts those beautiful trees down. But while I can remember the past, I can't control the future. We did the best we could to remember her.

The wild flower garden that Joy planted with seeds brought back from our vacation in Vermont the previous summer. Bob built the flower box.

The cedar swing set and playhouse that entertained Sarah and her friends for many summer days. It's now overgrown with weeds.

watering it and seeing it slowly grow over the next four years. After first assuming that it had grown too large for me to move by myself—which was the reality for me—I brooded awhile about it.

Then one sunny June day, again in 2006—Father's Day, in fact—I decided that my lovely Japanese maple was going to say "sayonara" to our old house and I went back to fetch it. Armed with shovels of different sizes, a sturdy eight-foot long two-by-four and a four-wheeled dolly to roll it over to my truck, parked some twenty yards away on the edge of our former property, I stood before the purple object of my affection to brace myself for the task I had chosen to undertake.

The little Asian tree was somewhat larger, and I was now four years older, at fifty-six; but I dug away all the heavy, moist dirt surrounding it, going as deeply as I could to sever all the many thin roots that the tenacious tree had sent out to securely anchor itself over the last few years. Then, after I had isolated the essential ball of roots—as much as I felt was safe for the tree but still possible for me to move—I wedged my heavy eight-foot long two-by-four between the bottom of the root ball and the dark wet earth at the bottom of the hole. Using the metal dolly as the pivot for my lever, I slowly elevated the tree out of that hole, carefully pressing my one hundred seventy pounds on the far end of the lever so that I didn't slip, because if I *did* slip, that would suddenly release my heavy plant from one end of the springy two-by-four causing the other end to bounce up and slap me across the wide grassy yard with unknown possible injuries.

But after an hour, I was successful in wrestling that prize of mine out of the earth, onto the cart and into my truck, where it laid passively on its side, probably muttering curses at me, in leafy Japanese, for disturbing its tranquility.

With my long experience in compensating for my advancing age, I was able to do it without really exhausting myself or doing any harm to the tree, I hoped. Once back at my new home, I unloaded it with the endless advice and eventual assistance of my sturdy nine-year-old daughter, Sarah. She had been just nine months old when we moved into that old house in May 1997. Now she was replanting one of its trees with me, pouring water all around it and patting rich, black dirt firmly into place on every side of the trunk with her strong little hands. I watched her do this work with total absorption of her task.

Things change.

****

My grandfather, Nathan Warman from Byelorussia, used to tell me that we all made our own luck. I muse about that sometimes.

I think that some people, mostly prosperous people in secure situations, believe that life offers them a package deal of "healthy, wealthy *and* wise," like the good luck in this world is a kind of buffet and a person can pick all they can carry on their tray.

But to me, overwhelmed by experience, I believe that the reality is "healthy, wealthy *or* wise," not all three. In my case, I missed out on the first two, and want to believe I received the last one as a consolation prize. I think, to a degree, that good fortune is created by the choices one makes. Not all that one sees in the world of the apparently successful may be what meets the eye. There can be fatal cracks in the foundation under the Golden Mansion.

The sexy trophy wife may have enough beauty and curves to melt a guy's eyes but may also be missing a few essentials, like say, a heart and soul, which generally become more evident during the eventual divorce. Pampered and endlessly indulged young children who never lack for anything, drowning in the latest and most fashionable clothes, toys, schools, vacations and frequently, therapists, may grow up disconnected from the reality most people struggle with, and unmotivated to make something of themselves.

If everything a child points to is immediately available to them, why should they ever have to sweat to attain something? The very concept of working toward a goal may be foreign to them. And possibly, the very busy, very social parents bestowing a never-ending conveyer belt of expensive things toward their impatiently waiting children—everything except the parent's own very limited time and attention—may find those grown-up children one day leaving their well-padded nest, easily shedding their unearned bounty of possessions and also…Sorry Mom! Sorry, Dad!…their distant, indifferent and busy parents. They can't miss someone they don't really know, can they?

I know what money can't buy. It can't buy the loving, attentive, beautiful children Joyce and I have raised. It can't make them love each other, and choose to seek each other out, as they frequently do. It can't make them all amazingly, artistically and musically talented, but they are. We told each of them,

"We don't care if you fail at making a living using whatever art you choose to pursue. But we *do* care very much…that at least you gave it a *chance*."

With solid emotional support like that, kids are willing to give all kinds of things a try. In our little group, it has produced a terrific singer with a band, a filmmaker who has been flown to Asia and Europe, and an occupational therapist who when she finally decided to make time for her talent, produced clay sculptures that are widely admired and are on sale in a local art gallery. Young Sarah draws constantly. She hears our praise for her clever use of color, endlessly. She beams with pleasure, every time. Who knows where she'll go with her art? Sarah knowing that her eventual decision will be fine with us, is all she *needs* to know.

Will they make millions from what they chose to express themselves? Most likely not, but that was never the driving force that made us want to give them the gift of richer cultural lives. We gave them time. We gave them attention and encouragement. Money was never the motivation or the goal. Self-expression was the whole point. With the reassurance that artistic failure *is* an acceptable possibility, kids are liable to try anything. Being content with your abilities is a gift in and of itself.

****

When I first met Joyce, over thirty years ago, she was a total knockout. I fell in love with her and never recovered. Somewhere along the way, I started telling her that I loved her, every day, twice.

Every morning and every night (if I die before I wake, etc...I wasn't taking any chances). I also tell her *all* the time, that she's beautiful.

Well, as of this writing, Joy is fifty-six. She's had a couple of C-sections, nearly thirty years ago, to make it possible for her to give birth to the singer and the filmmaker; and a few years ago, she was diagnosed with multiple sclerosis.

Many superficial things change when events and conditions like those above assault a woman's body. So very often, when I tell Joy that I still think she's beautiful, she gives me a *"What's wrong with you anyway?"* kind of look, and then mutters at me, dismissively,

"Yeah, yeah, sure..."

What Joyce doesn't get, or apparently believe, is that after being with her for so many years, I see the totality of her, not just the sometimes cruel effects of time and illness. I see who she is as a person, what she capable of doing, what she's accomplished over the decades, the fights she fought by my side and also for herself, the kind of mother she is and how she makes me feel when she smiles that dynamite smile at me.

She cynically suggests I'm full of crap when I tell her she's beautiful, or when I so often tell her I love her, but if I stopped saying either, after a time, she'd feel it.

In the world of values and relationships I inhabit, these feelings I have for her are also things money could never buy. No one could ever pay me to tell someone, anyone, that I loved them, if I did not. And one day, Joy may actually comprehend that in *her* case, no one could possibly find enough dollars to ever force me to stop.

****

So, how do I feel about the inhuman corporate automatons that wouldn't return our calls, wouldn't give us a break and cared nothing for the devastation that befell my fragile family when we all became just a negative cash producing numerical entity to be transferred from one balance sheet to the next?

Well...if ever I read this story to young children, I'd say to them:

"Y'know kids, ya gotta be tough in life. Ya gotta roll with the punches. Sometimes you win...and sometimes...people come and take your house away."

But if I'm talking to grownups, real world people like me with beating hearts and scary lives who know what savage things money can make some people do to other people, well...

I'd like to say I'm not really angry or bitter, but I'm a total failure at lying. Losing my house was like having my lungs torn out of my body. And as far as the people who made the decision to do that to me, to my wife and to my children?

One lovely Summer day, I hope they all gather together on a terrace at their corporate headquarters, to take the time to savor life, to smell all the colorful, fragrant flowers. And when they are collectively at the height of their inner peace and tranquility,

...I hope all their fucking heads explode.

****

So, I went back to the house I used to own the morning after I received the notice informing me our house was sold, to take one more look around and see if I forgot anything I might still want to take to our new place. I was given thirty days to clear out.

Thoughtful of them to grant us so much time.

I unlocked the kitchen door where the St. Bernard had come bounding into my life six months before, and I slowly walked around, peering into every room, remembering the people who lived in those rooms and the things that had happened there.

Then I poked into a crawl space under the sloping roof, through a door off of a large closet that Joy and I had converted into "Sarah's

Office." I had one, Joyce had one, so to little Sarah's logical mind, *she* should have one, too. I built shelves in there for all her books, and also built in a desk to hold her own computer. I even had an electrician put lights in that would shine over her shoulders when she wanted to read in there. It was very cozy, and Sarah loved her little office.

Inside the dark and dusty crawl space, I found an overlooked box of toys, photographs and drawings that belonged to Sarah's older sister, Rachel, when she was much younger. Then I went down to my musty office in the basement, and carefully removed a flexible, antique fluorescent light fixture that had belonged to a ninety year-old Lithuanian-Jewish master diamond cutter who was a friend of my mother's, when she was still designing jewelry, in the early Fifties.

I found a long steel spike, left over from when I built Joy's wildflower box...sixteen feet by eight feet...now in full bloom. We planted five pounds of wildflower seeds that we brought back with us when we took a long trip to visit rustic, mountainous Vermont, years ago.

Then, I went into the two-car garage and found stacks of 1920s *National Geographics* sitting on the damp concrete floor. I had no use for them any longer; but I took them anyway on general principals, getting soaked in the process from a sudden thunderstorm, as I loaded them into my minivan.

Then, I let my eyes cast about in the gloom of the garage that was filled with all sorts of things we could not possibly squeeze into our modest new home. So we just left them there, in resignation. Suddenly, over in a corner, covered with old tarps, a tent and partly covered by a moldy mattress, I saw a forgotten buried treasure.

Pulling all that dusty junk away from it, I stood back to admire my long ago handiwork. It was a large wooden castle that I built for my three now grown-up children when they were still little and I was unemployed, in Winter 1985.

Over a period of thirty days, I used bits and pieces of spare lumber and hardware scattered around my workshop, and I constructed a three-dimensional, interactive castle, four feet wide by five feet tall. Life-size for my kids, at that time. It was modeled after the Aladdin's Castle that I loved to explore in Chicago's long gone and simply fantastic Riverview Amusement Park, which ran alongside the murky North Branch of the Chicago River.

It even had a resident dragon that had an articulated neck that twisted and turned and could swiftly attack the unsuspecting through some of the castle's many windows.

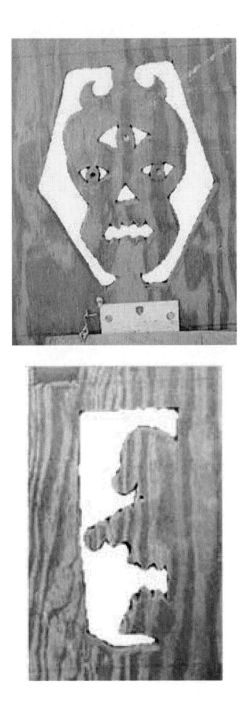

I gazed at the long forgotten handmade family heirloom, far too big to fit somehow into my much smaller situation, and I remembered what it meant to me to be able to give my young kids something that no other father could give his children for Chanukah...or Christmas either, for that matter. Other kids could come look at it, and play with it, but they could not own it. Only *my* kids could.

I walked over to it and ran my hand over its many carved windows, shelves and gargoyles, just letting the seconds flow by, with the thunder from the rainstorm filling my ears, knowing that it was not takeable...and I wavered in my emptiness. Then, deciding, I walked out of the dark garage and through the heavy rain to the trunk of my minivan.

I quickly grabbed a Phillips screwdriver in the toolbox I always carried with me and walked back into the garage. I began unscrewing the three screws that attached the base of the dragon's neck to the castle, one by one, letting the old screws just fall to the floor until the still very flexible wooden dragon dropped, into my waiting hand.

I held it up in front of me, gently tilting it, letting it swing this way and that, to see how well it worked...the same way I did over twenty years ago when I first created it, much like how Pinocchio sprang to life out of odd pieces of hand carved wood.

The dragon's angry head kind of bobbed and weaved...the colors I painted it in 1985 to make it look so fierce...now faded, but still there, and I said to myself, out loud as if that long forgotten castle could actually hear me,

"I guess...just *this*...will have to do."

Then holding the flexible dragon and the screwdriver in one hand, I walked out of what used to be my garage, pressed the button to lower the heavy overhead door one last time, watching my castle disappear as the door fell...separating me from that house...forever.

I got into my car and backed out of the cracked asphalt driveway, through the torrents of wind and rain, and I quietly drove away.

Part IV:

Damn it
Damn it!
Damn it!
Damn it!
Damn it!
Damn it!
Damn it!
Damn it!
Damn it!
Damn it!
Damn it!
Damn it!
Damn it!
Damn it!
Damn it!
Damn it!
Damn it!
Damn it!
Damn it!
Damn it!
Damn it!

Part V:
Our Castle's Reign Restored!
Its Fiery Dragon Reunited!

All through the next two nights, I struggled with my strangely uncharacteristic willingness to surrender something so valuable to me.

Although there was so much I could do nothing about, the castle took on a symbolic meaning to me that transcended practicality, and if I could summon a little imagination, and some gumption, this frustrating story might have a different ending.

Just because the moment with a huge and mysterious St. Bernard, five months earlier had taken on a fairy tale quality that now seemed silly to me as time passed, my wooden castle was very real and part of my family's history. Why let it go?

The black night sky slowly gave birth to a new day's glow.

I felt my mood gradually shift from defeated powerlessness to renewed resolution.

I *knew* there was a way I could do this.

I threw the covers off of me and silently slipped out of my bed, so I wouldn't wake up my sleeping wife. Our three sleeping dogs stirred a bit, but it was too early for them, too. Betsy the Beagle opened one eye and glared at me, as if to say,

"Do you mind?"

I scratched behind her ears. She closed her eye and snuggled closer to my hand with a doggy moan of pleasure. It worked every time.

I swiftly dressed and went into my office to find a plastic stack of drawers, like the ones they sell at the office supply stores. The plastic is almost clear and I could see the contents in the drawers without opening them. In a couple of seconds I found it and opened one of the drawers. Inside was the long-necked Dragon I'd disconnected from the Castle a couple of days before, after **twenty years** of their being attached to each other. It lay on its side and looked so mournful. That only strengthened my resolve. I picked up the Castle's guardian, now so alone in the otherwise empty drawer, and looked into its wooden eye.

"Come on, Dragon. We're gonna go get the Mother Ship!"

Was that a smile I detected? It was so early in the morning, I really couldn't be sure.

I grasped the Dragon's fierce head in my hand, its long neck trailing behind me as I raced down the stairs and out the door. No mini-van today. No, *today* I would take the enormous, the cavernous, the gas-gulping huge box-on-wheels, my bright red and black 1990 Chevy Beauville Van.

If that bright red and black baby could handle a sectional couch, if it could move our large capacity Sears refrigerator, then surely it could swallow the heavy, but very slim, four foot by five foot rectangle that was my Castle.

Within ten minutes, I was backing into the driveway of a house I said I'd never return to. So much for *dramatic* exits. I pulled up close to the garage door and then jumped out and punched the code into the key pad, attached to the outside wall, that would make the door rise. While the heavy door made its familiar groan as it lifted back and up on its metal tracks into the garage, I made a beeline to the dark corner where my brooding, abandoned Castle sat, awaiting its unknown fate.

Would it land upside down, crushed in a dumpster? Would wreckers chop it up and feed it to the fieldstone fireplace inside my house, and watch its old, dry wood burst into flames? Would anyone care that they were watching more than one hundred hours of my hand-carving go up in smoke and sparks, flowing toward heaven through the house's brick chimney?

Not *today*, baby. I stood in front of its heavy self. You're coming home with me. I placed one hand under its left turret and my other hand under its right turret. Then I took a deep breath, kept my fragile back straight up and down and with a grunt, lifted that slab of a toy up in the air and walked as quickly as a guy could, under those conditions, toward the two already opened back doors of my big red and black van.

I don't know how much that massive thing weighed, but I sure was glad I hadn't carved a dungeon to go with it. Tilting it head first into the van at a forty-five degree angle, I gave the bottom of the Castle a mighty shove and it slid into the empty van like it was meant for it. Then I slammed the two big doors shut and turned to look at the garage, as if I really cared anymore. But grown-ups do grown-up things and I left my old house secured. The heavy garage door was slowly sinking back to Earth as I turned west out of the driveway.

The Dragon was lying between the two front seats of the van, its ferocious head facing back toward the top of the Castle. Was that a fire-breathing greeting I smelled as I climbed back into the van? Hard to say. I hadn't had much contact with that old Dragon for a long, long time.

While driving back to my new place, I was desperately trying to come up with a reason my wife would agree to let me keep this big thing inside the smaller house.

It depended on her mood. It depended on the stars. I had no idea what I would say to Joy about what I was planning to bring into her home. Inside every peaceable Norwegian is a wild, raging, ax-swinging Viking, bursting to break out. I had to be careful with Joy. And her inner warrior, too.

Joy heard me back up the van into our driveway, aiming toward the front door. Evidently curious about where I'd run off to so early in the morning, she was waiting to see what wonderful surprise I had brought back for her. She crept closer to the van's back windows and peered inside.

"*Forget it*," she announced. "You're not bringing that miserable hunk of slivers inside *my* clean house."

Then she turned abruptly and stalked back inside. *Not* a good beginning, I thought to myself. Apparently we didn't share the same sense of what was an irreplaceable treasure and family heirloom. I looked down at the faded Dragon head resting between the seats and said to it, fondly,

"This may take some time. Please, be patient."

I saw nothing unusual about talking to a dead piece of wood. I knew that *another* wooden response was waiting for me, inside the house.

It took a week to get Joy to listen to me.

Annoyed Norwegians have a unique way of arguing.

They say...*nothing*.

Not one word.

A big argument in Norway would truly be the "sound of silence."

But I wheedled and pleaded and explained that it wasn't *really* a toy at all. Why, it was actually Middle-American folk art...and that there ought to be a place of honor for it on our walls, where we could proudly display it to our friends and relatives.

My blond...was *not* amused.

So I rubbed her feet, cuddled her and told her how much it meant to me. I could feel her resolve beginning to crack. I decided this possible crumbling of the granite would require a lot more foot rubbing. After ice cream and flowers were added to my campaign, the Viking Queen relented, and put away her deadly ax. I could breathe now. Gotta be careful with those Norwegians. Flowing blond hair and dreamy blue eyes were but a thin veneer, barely covering the smoldering danger that lurked within them.

We finally agreed that it would go on a wall, of *her* choosing, of course. This would take more time. My Castle sat in its Chevy tomb for another week. I guess...I did have a dungeon after all. At last Joy selected a wall—a good space where the sun would shine on my wooden baby. It was very clever, and typical of her. Not a spot I would have picked. But still, she had a question:

"Bob, how will you keep it attached to the wall?"

I replied, "Oh, I'll find a good strong stud...and then screw it into the wall."

A pause occurred.

Then Joy looked at me, with a sly smile,

"Are we still talking about...the Castle?"

Another pause.

Why, this was so sudden!

Then she began walking upstairs and turned to give me one of her alluring, Norwegian maiden "come hither" looks. So I followed her up the stairs. I should probably mention that at fifty-six, any expression *whatsoever* on her face is considered by me to be a "come hither" look...including hysteria and indigestion.

I don't see as well as I used to, so I don't want to miss any possible opportunities.

As I was thoughtfully climbing the stairs, I got this cool idea for *another* story about this **incredibly huge, fire-breathing dragon,** about the size of, oh, Texas!...and who was *really, really* pissed at this...**Evil Mortgage Company...**

I guess I can work on it later.

"Hey, *Joy*...?"

****

Good-night, people.

Be *very* quiet.

My Dragon is home now...and he sleeps.

The Castle's first owner, King David, hands it over to its new owner, Queen Sarah.

The Dragon was very pleased.

...here is the little bit of Christine that I treasure and never dreamed I would ever write about.

The details may surprise you; but not anything about the character of Chris will be news to any of you that knew her. And...if a stranger who never knew her should ever read these words, some day, let me tell you about someone really wonderful. Someone with a heart.

8

Losing Christine

This is all wrong.

These words should never be hitting this paper.

There's just no way that I could live longer than Christine.

In my mind, in my heart, she's still fifteen, sixteen years old, damn it.

I didn't even know her very well.

I don't know her middle name, if she even had one, or her birthday, or what her mother looked like...none of that. But our lives crossed paths, twice, when it really meant something to me, and I owe it to Chris, to her friends—some of whom are also my friends, for a lifetime—and well, for myself, too, to write this down about her, so we can all have just a few more moments with her, to help us all bear the shock and the terrible pain of her sudden death.

She wasn't my girlfriend. She was part of a loosely formed bunch of friends that originally went to Bowen High School, on the South Side of Chicago, in the late Sixties. Now I read that the City is tearing down old Bowen...one more piece of our collective past collapsing into broken brick, twisted steel and ancient dust.

I didn't go to Bowen. I went to the private Lab School in Hyde Park, miles away. But almost everyone I cared about...even after four years at my own high school...went to Bowen.

So, for sweet, round, funny Carol Fineberg, serious and mysterious Bob Lachata, eternally sexy (and very smart) Suzy Fox, assorted husbands and wives who became part of us, Dina Hauser... who was nice to me very long ago, when not many girls were, other friends that joined our many reunions over the last thirty years whose names I don't remember, and finally for Rick Munden, who became the heart of our group whenever he flew back to us from California and Steve Shoub, who married, loved and cared for Christine for thirty-five years...here is the little bit of Christine that I treasure and never dreamed I would ever write about.

The details may surprise you, but not anything about the character of Chris will be news to any of you. And...if strangers who never knew her should ever read these words, some day, let me tell you about someone really wonderful. Someone with a heart.

****

Rick and I opened a newsstand in August of 1965. I needed the money to pay for my high school tuition, but even though the newsstand became gradually more successful, for Rick, it was a way station to the next place he wanted to be. So, after he left the stand in December 1966, sometimes he would come by to visit me, and he brought this very quiet girl with him. Christine.

She was skinny, kind of tall, had very long, blond hair and large, intelligent eyes. But I thought she was shy, because she never said much, the few times I saw her. And some time went by. Then one day, about a year later, Rick brought Christine with him again and I wasn't sure it was the same girl. Nature had kicked in...and Christine was a knockout. I thought to myself,

"Man, Rick, you can sure pick 'em!"

But only to myself.

Later, in early June 1968, I was in the part of Chicago where I got my braces tightened every couple of weeks, and I dropped by this restaurant where I knew Christine was working as a waitress. I was pretty glum that day. I just went there to say hello.

My girlfriend, Barbara, had come down with the measles and would not be able to go to my Senior Prom with me. She was the only girl I'd ever dated in four years at Lab School, and now she was unavailable for the one event I wanted to attend, in a school where I wasn't popular, and never went to any dances. Besides, being eighteen with braces, I was not such a catch. Girls didn't see me in the hallways...and swoon.

After I got the news of Barb's illness, I first decided to just forget about the Prom...bad luck happens. Then I thought it over and changed my mind. I'd find someone else to go with me. There had to be lots of girls without dates. So, using the yearbook as a guide to which girl was which, and the school directory that listed all the students and their home phone numbers (don't *all* high schools hand those things out to *everyone*?), I started calling girls. And getting turned down. And calling more girls. And getting turned down.

NO, no, NO, no, NO, no, NO, no, NO, no, NO, no, NO, no, NO, no...and NO!

I'll save you the trouble of counting all those **NO's**.

Seventeen.

Seventeen girls I knew for four years all said...**NO!**...to me.

Long after any sane boy would admit to defeat, and accept his total social rejection, I kept calling. I don't give up so easily. But then, I'm not that smart, either.

But finally, I did give up and settled for just feeling bad. When Chris saw me, dressed in her white waitress uniform, looking better than any of the seventeen girls who told me to go fly a kite, she came over to say hello. She was always friendly to me.

She must have seen my downcast face, and unenthusiastic reply to her greeting, and figured something was wrong. She'd never seen me looking so dejected before. Well, having *seventeen* girls deem you unworthy as a date for the Senior Prom can pretty much devastate a fella's self-esteem. So, as candidly as I would tell a guy, because I didn't think of Chris as anything else but a friend, I told her my sad story. Without interrupting, she listened.

Then, silence.

She was standing next to the table where I was sitting, like she was taking an order for dinner. Then she said,

"Bob, listen, don't feel so bad. *I'll* go with you to the Prom."

More silence.

I looked up at her pretty face, with it's serious eyes and stared at Christine for a long moment. Girls that looked like *her*....did *not* go to proms with guys like...*me*.

Incredulous, I said to her,

"Chris, c'mon, you're not serious......"

But she was, and replied,

"Bob, why miss this thing you want to do just because your girlfriend got sick. Here's my phone number, and address..."

And she quickly wrote them down on a napkin and handed it to me.

"Tell me the date and time and come pick me up. It'll be cool. We'll have a good time and you'll get to go to your Prom. I gotta go, I have a customer."

Then she walked away and left me sitting there, confused. Why would she do a thing like that?

I got up, and walked uncertainly toward the door. Then I turned to say goodbye. Chris was busy waiting on someone, but she looked up, saw me, smiled and waved. I smiled back at her. My face would get used to looking happier.

I called the place where I had reserved a tuxedo, and cancelled my prior cancellation. The guy there thought it was hilarious.

I picked Christine up at her house the night of the Prom. She was dazzling. She kissed me on my cheek, like I was a *real* date. I sheepishly gave the corsage to her, unwilling to attempt to pin it to the thin fabric covering her chest. Girls that looked like Chris didn't go to proms with guys that looked like me.

Later, at the Sheraton-Chicago in Downtown Chicago, on ritzy North Michigan Avenue, I suddenly realized that my classmates, including many of the *No's*, thought the same thing as me. I could see it in their eyes. The amazed disbelief. This was better than a movie. It was real.

We danced. We had dinner. I lost my cummerbund. It was a great night.

When the Prom was over, I drove Christine back to her house. I opened the car door and held her hand as she got out. Then I walked with her to the front door.

She kissed me goodnight, not on the cheek. Like it was a real date. I was enchanted.

Then she said goodnight to me, with her big beautiful smile, her long blond hair spilling over her shoulders and, just like Cinderella at Midnight...she disappeared.

And with that last kiss, those seventeen terrible *No's* all went up in smoke.

Magic, Christine.

Magic.

****

I didn't see Chris again for six months, not until the very end of December 1968.

It wasn't exactly a happy reunion.

At least, not for me.

****

I'd been having severe headaches for years, on the left side of my head, above my ear. I could remember having them as far back as when I was eight, in 1958.

Though my parents took me to various specialists to try to figure out what was wrong, no one was able to help me. Looking back from 2006, medicine as practiced then was vastly more primitive than now, especially in the area of diagnosis, in my case.

So I was basically told to just live with it, since no one could find any way to stop the periodic sharp pain in my head. Years passed, and the headaches grew more intense and closer together than when I was a child. But between working at my newsstand seven days a week and trying to survive and graduate from an exceptionally demanding high school, within the grounds of the University of Chicago, I didn't have time for the luxury of seeking out ever more doctors to tell me they had no idea how to help me.

Then, in late September 1968, right after I began my freshman (and only) year at the University of Illinois in Chicago, I was driving my van through Hyde Park, where my newsstand was. While waiting for a red light to turn green, I blacked out in traffic.

I woke up in the middle of the intersection, where my car had slowly rolled through the red light, maybe twenty or thirty seconds later. I heard horns blaring and brakes screeching as the cars and trucks entering the intersection tried to avoid smashing into my barely moving van. No one hit me and I quickly regained control of my car and drove to my apartment without any more trouble. I had no clue as to what happened to me.

I considered myself lucky that no cops had witnessed the incident and that I had escaped an expensive ticket, for effectively "running" through a red light. In the weeks to come, however, the concept of what was "lucky" was to take on a radically different meaning.

My story is about remembering Christine and not about my complicated medical history, so I won't relate the long series of doctors, beginning with the clinic in the University of Illinois that eventually landed me in St. Francis Hospital in Evanston, Illinois. There, on December 20, 1968, a well known and respected surgeon named Dr. Slaughter, removed most of my left jawbone, after it was determined that I had, and always had, for more than a decade, salivary gland cancer.

All this was done on my Christmas vacation, so I didn't miss a minute of school. I was sent home on the morning of December 31, New Year's Eve.

I was living in South Shore, in a modest apartment on the second floor, facing Lake Michigan. I sat in a soft old chair, staring out the window, watching the waves roll in, over and over, hypnotically. The pain drugs were very strong, along with antibiotics and whatever else I was supposed to take for weeks to come.

My neck had a large padded bandage taped to my skin, covering about a quarter of my face, which was paralyzed on the left side, temporarily, they told me. My weight had dropped from a robust 150 pounds to about 130, and I had lost quite a bit of blood. I was very weak, very tired and completely alone. It was New Year's Eve and I was going...*nowhere.*

I sat in that soft chair for hours, dozing off and on, feeling very sorry for myself, watched those endless waves, and stared at the sky as it turned black over the lake, after the early Winter sunset. My future prospects were unknown, and my surgeon, an honest man, had offered me no rosy guarantees of being free from further surgery in the years to come. The sky may have been very dark, but not as black as my mood. I felt empty and very tired.

Then the loud buzzer, on the intercom near my front door, went off. I debated whether to try to get up to answer it. Probably just a mistake anyway...nobody knew I was coming to my home that day. But I had nothing else to do, so I dragged myself over to the intercom to see if someone was still down there.

"Who's there?" I croaked through the lumpy bandages that muffled my speech.

"Christine," a young woman's voice responded. "Can I come up?"

I was confused, trying to remember, mumbling to myself:

First: *"Christine?"*

Then: *"Chris...tine..."*

Then, at last: ***"Christine!"***

I urgently pressed the button and whispered, in my amazement, "Yes. Please come up."

After graduation, everybody in my group of friends scattered to wherever they were going, to celebrate escaping high school, except for me, leashed to my newsstand. For months, I didn't see anyone or know who was moving away, or what was happening. The old crowd has dispersed, and I figured, well, it had to happen some day...

Though I thought about my wonderful prom night with Chris for a while, after it happened, work and college eventually left all that in my past. I wasn't going to call her again. I knew it was a one-time thing, just a favor, really, and I resumed my relationship with my girlfriend. But she and I kind of ran out of steam, after a few more months. So now, I had no one. With the endless procession of doctors closing in on what was wrong with me, my social life disappeared.

How could Chris even know about all this stuff? I was mystified, but so very happy just to hear her voice.

When she knocked on the door, I was waiting, leaning on it, and quickly opened it to see her. She was wearing an old, warm-looking, long brown leather coat, jeans and a T-shirt, her long blond hair splashing all around the collar of the coat. She looked at me, too, but wisely, she chose to lie. She told me how good I looked, considering, and gave me a delicate hug, like I might break if she squeezed me too hard.

Maybe I would.

If she was "Cinderella," as I imagined her the last time I saw her on the night of the prom, I had no illusions that I was her, or anyone's, Prince Charming. But medicine can come in a variety of containers. Why, I was feeling better...already!

Chris hooked her arm through mine, and walked me over to my couch, away from the window where I'd been sitting all day. She seemed to know what to do. She was only in the door for a minute, and somehow....sized up the situation immediately.

I settled into the couch, opposite her, when my curiosity couldn't be suppressed any longer.

"How did you know...?" My voice trailed off in wonder.

"Carol," Chris replied, matter-of-factly.

"Oh." And I knew immediately.

Carol Fineberg, a Jewish mother even as a teenager, was the one person who was still around and I must have run into her and told her what was going to happen, a couple days before the surgery. To my total surprise, the evening before I was to go to the hospital in the morning, Carol came over to my apartment, unasked, to spend the night cuddling with me. She told me she didn't want me to wake up alone to such a scary situation. This wasn't about sex. But it was about love. And friendship.

How could it be that I deserved friends like these? Sometimes, you don't know when you're rich beyond all expectations. But I was learning.

Chris hung up her coat and looked around the apartment to see where things were. Then she asked me if I was hungry and without waiting for a reply, perhaps noticing how easy it was for her to feel my ribs through my shirt, when she first hugged me, she rummaged through my refrigerator and kitchen, and made dinner for both of us. I couldn't open my mouth more than an inch, what with the titanium wires transplanted to where the jawbone had been, but whatever she made was miles—no, *eons*—better than the flavorless hospital gruel I'd endured for the last two weeks.

So while I tried to eat without making a sloppy mess of myself, Chris talked about this and that, never remarking on the way I was eating or looked. She created a warm reality that made me very comfortable. I wasn't there to impress the girl. She was there, I realized, to take care of me.

After a while, when I remembered what day it was, I asked her,

"Don't you have a date, or something, for New Year's Eve, Chris?"

She was cleaning up the dishes, and brushed off my question with a brief,

"I want to be here, okay?"

Yeah, that was okay. I decided to be taken care of. No more dumb questions.

But the way that girl looked, she could have gone anywhere she wanted to go, that night. I was slow to understand how such a beautiful girl could be so caring for someone who was *not* her special love, instead of letting older guys with nice cars fawn all over her, like I was used to seeing at my privileged high school, where girls like Christine didn't exist.

The evening crept by. We talked some...watched TV...I dozed... she made sure I took my many medicines...she made tea...and she snuggled close to me on the couch.

I must have been sleeping, because I felt myself being gently shaken. When I opened my eyes, I saw Chris's lovely face, close to mine, smiling her smile.

"Bob, it's 1969! *Happy New Year!*"

And she kissed me.

Why, hello again...Cinderella.

Then she told me she had to go. That she told some friends she'd meet them after midnight, but she didn't want me to spend New Year's Eve all alone, the same day I came home from the hospital. So she thought I would feel better if she spent the evening with me, instead. She said it tenderly, leaving no doubt that being there with me was what she really wanted to do.

I told her she was an Angel. Not *my* Angel. Just *an* Angel.

She smiled that smile at me again, wished me better luck in the New Year, and then she was gone, taking her fairy dust with her.

No, no...she was really just *my* angel...and I fell back asleep.

****

But a *different* fairy tale 'spell' took over, after that night.

More like **Rip Van Winkel** than Cinderella.

I didn't see Christine again...for *sixteen* years.

****

My dad, Irving, had a group of really close pals from the old Jewish West Side of Chicago, a dozen men born in 1912, 1913.

One of his closest friends, someone I saw many times as a child and later as an adult, was Larry Schoub. They were like brothers. They loved each other. Their parents, from the Jewish Pale in Eastern Europe, knew each other.

My dad got a call one day, in March, 1984, that Larry had died, after a long illness, at seventy-one. Even though we had both visited Larry in the hospital, as his condition worsened, his death was like a hammer blow to my father. He found an old box buried in his closet, filled with pictures of his pals from the West Side. He rummaged through it, his lips tightly pressed together, it seemed to me, to keep from screaming...I watched him cry, his shoulders shaking, as I tried to comfort him. He was in such pain, I could feel it myself, as I wrapped my arms around him and he cried on my shoulder.

We went to the funeral together, and I was surprised to see the door to the chapel open, and out walked...Christine! An older, more serious Christine, now thirty-two.

Right behind her was someone I had never met, Larry's nephew, Steve Shoub. Chris introduced me, we all shook hands, but I was still amazed at our meeting. Chris was married to Steve, since November 1971. A coincidence, I thought. I was married in June 1971. Seeing them together, it was like she was now part of my family as well. Steve came across to me as a warm and gentle man, much like his Uncle Larry.

We only spoke for a moment. I had to get back to my store after the memorial service. But I learned that Chris was attending The University of Illinois, at the Chicago Campus, studying medicine. She was also a certified auto mechanic, an obviously related field. Her handshake was considerably firmer than in 1968, and the skin not as soft. I could feel the calluses on her palm, but it wasn't something I would talk about.

Driving back to my store from the memorial service, I had an uneasy feeling about Chris, and how she was doing. She had that look in her eyes. With my own, by then, many more surgeries and hospital stays since that major one in late December, 1968—some voluntary...some not—I knew when someone had endured too much pain for too long.

About two years earlier, in 1982, I'm not certain of the date, Chris called me one night at my home in Evanston, Illinois. I didn't know how she found my phone number. We had not spoken to each other since New Year's Eve, 1968. She was living in Florida with Steve. Despite my surprise at hearing her voice, I sensed from the tone of her voice that this wasn't a call to remember old times.

Chris was in pain, and she was frightened. She had developed osteomylitis in her jaw and there seemed to be no relief from the pain and the degradation of the bone. She was talking fast and her voice seemed quite a bit lower than when I last heard it.

She poured out her frustration and the details of her illness faster than I could absorb it. Her descriptions were very detailed and technical, but I didn't want to interrupt her, even though I had trouble keeping up with the rapid-fire recounting of the misery she had experienced. She wasn't calling me to chat, or to discuss her scary situation.

I eventually realized that she had a deep need to pour all this out, and for some reason she had tracked me down, so that I, in particular, would hear her story. She talked to me for almost an hour. Then I figured it out. Of all the people she might have described her situation to, perhaps only *I* had a *real* comprehension of what it meant to lose a jaw, as she was frightened that she might lose one, too. Maybe my continued survival gave her hope. I can't prove that was her reason for calling me. But I still believe it, today.

I didn't have a whole lot to say, or much opportunity to say it, with the torrent of her words coming at me through the phone. I tried to tell her not to despair...that new and more effective drugs were being developed all the time...that I had learned to cope with my own chronic pain and physical complications...and that my life was mostly normal. I couldn't hold Chris in my arms and comfort her, the way I would when one of my three small children skinned a knee or lost a tooth. But, man...I wanted to.

The last time we met, *I* was the one being tenderly comforted, by her. Now, strangely, sadly, things had flipped. I was very grateful to be someone she would call to pour her heart out to. It mattered very much to me, that I might be of some use to this wonderful woman. But I wished it could some *other* kind of use of me. Perhaps talking to me gave her some temporary relief, an outlet she knew she'd be listened to by someone uniquely qualified to hear her story. I can only hope that is true. She didn't volunteer that to me, nor did she ever call me again, in the remaining twenty-four years of her life. But she did thank me for listening, before saying goodnight and goodbye.

After Christine's call, I stood silently in my office, still holding the phone, still feeling a link to her, not wanting to let it go...not yet.

Then, the spell breaking, I thought it over and decided to call "The Leader of the Pack," Rick Munden. I thought he'd want to know what Chris was going through. I knew that he'd care.

Rick was very quiet when I delivered my sad news about his long ago girlfriend. I was sure I was doing the right thing, calling him about her. I didn't know if Chris had already called him, before she called me, but the surprise in his hushed voice after hearing about her illness and pain answered my unasked question.

I gave him the number she had given me before she hung up and told him I'd talk to him later. Usually, when we called each other, we'd talk for thirty minutes to an hour, but not this time.

I don't know if he called her.

It wasn't any of my business.

Rick and I never discussed it. Old relationships like theirs were very private, and did not include me. I was just the messenger and sorry to even be that.

Of the little news that I told Christine, the major item was that I remarried after my divorce in 1977. I told her that my second wife, Joyce, and the mother of two of my three children, was beautiful, with long blonde hair, a great smile, warm eyes and then...as I was telling her a bit more, I had this surreal feeling that my description of my wife, was an echo of a very similar description of someone else I could have given, about sixteen years before. But I never would say anything like that to Chris. She didn't need to hear that. But the echo stayed with me for a long time.

I did tell Chris that my second marriage was a good one, and that I was still very much in love with Joyce. Why did I say that? I don't know, frankly. But it is now twenty-four years later, and I know it was true then, because after our thirty-one years of being together, I am still very sure of it now.

Though Joyce and Christine never met, which I regret, they might've made good friends, as...similar...as they were, in many ways. Maybe one unfortunate reason would've been is that Joyce, too, has a very difficult medical situation. My wife has multiple sclerosis. And I do put my arms around her as often as she'll let me, to try and comfort her, when she is sad and in pain. But she does the same for me, and I am grateful for her care and love, every day.

****

In July, 2005, Rick Munden called a bunch of us from the old crowd and told us he wanted to come to Chicago to get together with everyone.

I had seen Rick many times when he came to Chicago, or I when went west to his state. One time, he drove across the desert in his ancient car to meet me in sizzling Las Vegas, Nevada at an American Booksellers Association Convention…when there used to be enough independent booksellers left to still have a convention. We always had things to talk about, interesting places to explore and both liked the pleasure of a good meal.

I had a world travel bookstore at the time, called Grand Tour, and I'd been to many places for conventions both in the USA and Europe. My feeling was, and continues to be, that if someone had lived their life in such a way as to please the Angels, as Rick was, they would be rewarded by being allowed to live in, or very near to, San Francisco, the coolest city in the United States.

Other people may have different opinions, but they are *all* wrong.

Rick maintained relationships with a wide range of people from many different backgrounds, was laid back and unpretentious, despite being very successful and respected in his high-tech work. He put people at ease, listened quietly to everyone's stories, and with his good sense of humor and easy laugh, made all kinds of people feel comfortable. I know all this, because I watched him interact with so many people over the forty-five years I've known him, and I wondered how he could be casual, affectionate and attentive to so many people at the same time. I decided that it was a gift.

He was also quietly sensitive to the ups and downs of his friends' fortunes, having experienced both conditions himself. When he would do something in that area, after recommending a good restaurant, usually Asian or Middle Eastern, that we should all meet at, it would be a surprise that when the bill for the exotic food and drink was due to come, it didn't come. It was already paid, without anyone noticing.

No flourishes, no grandstanding and not every time. Just when he felt it was the right time. Also, at no time when we gathered together, did the girls pay for anything. That was our collective chivalrous tradition, and we all liked playing our part as gentlemen. Even into our fifties, all the women were still "girls."

Rick became the magnet for a diverse group of his friends that did not always see each other in between his visits. I am not someone who is comfortable at parties, for example, but I would never miss a gathering of the old crowd from the South Side of Chicago. Like the lyric in an old Ricky Nelson song, "*…there was **magic** in the air…*"

So it was on a Monday, July 25, 2005, at 11 a.m. that our usual core crew, plus some new faces, showed up in the wonderfully recreated old Grant Park that was now known as "Millennium Park," with a Frank Geary designed band shell made of many hammered sheets of steel and his wavy wooden footbridge that crossed over Lake Shore Drive, with such a long and gentle inclination that people in wheelchairs could easily cross it. There was also an enormous, polished, mirror-like metal bean sculpture that a person could stand under or walk around and see themselves reflected in its skin. The park was full of artistic and architectural wonders for both children and adults. It was a grand success, after years and years of waiting for its completion, and it drew people to it from all over the world.

The day was warm, soon to be a scorcher, but the sky was so blue, filled with fluffy clouds and coasting birds, it was perfect. Like Rick had arranged it, from two thousand miles away.

When I arrived around ten or so, there were already a few couples there, sitting near an outside café. It was good to see them, old faces, still young to me, smiling in recognition at the approach of a friend met forty or more years before.

Rick, of course, Bob Lachata, Suzie Fox, Dina Hauser and her shaggy, lovable husband with his salt and pepper mane and beard, some friends of friends I didn't know but was happy to meet...people just drifted in from all over everywhere to join our growing circle of people who were instantly comfortable with each other.

We were going to find a restaurant to grab some lunch as it ticked toward noon, then go on an architectural boat ride on the Chicago River. It would be enjoyable, it would be outside and would easily accommodate physical problems any of the group may have had. It seemed that everyone was there that intended to be...and then, there was Christine. Christine...twenty-one years after I last saw her at Larry Shoub's funeral. Christine, who I hadn't seen since that indelible December in 1968, for no more than ten minutes, out of the last *thirty-seven years.*

I saw her before she saw me. She was with Steve, her husband I'd met with her at the funeral. I watched, silently, as they went from person to person, introducing Steve to her old friends and greeting them herself. She was so pale, so angular and thin, I couldn't get used to her now, as the glowing images of her from my memory crashed into the reality of the woman I saw today. It was hard for me to see the many fine lines on her face, lines I felt were etched there from the pain she had endured for so many years.

But worse, for me, was that I could hardly recognize her anymore. I wanted to see that girl who stayed with me the night when I came

Author's note: The following pictures show many of us in various combinations in Chicago's Grant Park and sailing in a river boat on the Chicago River. We were all very happy to be together, as you can see.

I won't name each person every time after I identify them in the beginning. I'll be using the maiden names of the women because I can't keep up with who's married and who's not. No offense intended.

Most of us have known each other for decades. I love all these people, and seeing all of us together for the last time on that sunny day is something I want to always remember.

From left, standing: Bob Katzman, Antoinette Ewing
From left, sitting: Rick Munden, Chris Shoub, Suzy Fox

Carol Feinberg standing on the left, Bobby Munden, Rick's son, sitting on the right.

The umbrellas were for the sun. It was a sizzlingly hot day on the Chicago River.

These pictures are from Rick. I can't find the roll I shot. There are great pictures on it of other places on the river and also places we stopped. I do not have pictures of Steve, Chris' husband, in this group, which I regret very much. When I find the pictures, I will print them. I know this is like a home movie, but it matters to me.

home from the hospital. I wanted to see that fairy tale princess I brought home from the Senior Prom. I wanted to see...Cinderella...

Chris...where did you go?

When she finally came around the circle of us, sitting around a table under a huge umbrella in the park, I rose to shake her smiling husband's hand, give Chris a quick hug and a kiss on her cheek, like she was anyone, just any old friend, and not someone who could still time stand still. You smile and say how wonderful they look...*isn't it amazing how you never seem to change?*...and then act like everything is as it always is, as the cracks start spreading through your heart.

Isn't that what old friends do? Give each other a magic mirror where they are eternally young and happy and their future is forever...?

How will I get through this day? *How* will I pretend for Christine?
Well…I will.
That's what old friends do.
They do impossible things…when they have to.

****

The day was perfect.

We didn't "grab" lunch somewhere. We went to a nice restaurant a couple of blocks away from the park, where the food was very good. People laughed easily at old jokes, comfortable with people that they may not have seen in decades, or people from their high school that they may have never met. Didn't matter. I guess…after fifty…people become more generous with each other.

I was a part of all of this, and I wasn't. I wasn't part of any of their Bowen High School memories. I didn't know any of the assorted teachers they remembered as horrible, easy, sexy…whatever…it was all just blanks to me. So while I was glad to be there with them, especially the core group of people I did know very well from my teens, in the Sixties, sometimes I just sat there and watched all of them rediscover each other.

Whatever passions the various girls may have stirred up in the guys there in the restaurant so many years before, and there was a mixture of former girlfriends and boyfriends, now it was just misty romantic recollections and a far greater concern for how every one was feeling…today.

We almost all wore glasses, had operations (I won the prize there, but didn't talk about it), lost one or more parents, had children that were either teens, grown up or, in my case, had an eight-year-old at home. The men were either becoming gray, or balding. The girls curves were well under control by now. Our differences were much less significant now, than our common experiences. This was better than being with my extended family. We were all here because we *wanted* to be here.

After lunch, we all slowly walked south down ritzy North Michigan Avenue toward the Chicago River, where the tourist boats were docked. Those of us that lived here, of course, never *ever* took the boat tours, so if it wasn't for the out-of-towners, we'd never experience some of the best times that Chicago could offer, on a sunny Summer day.

Once on the big white boat that leisurely drifted down the wide river, while the tour guide droned on about who designed *what* building, in *what* year, in a voice that I couldn't really hear very clearly, we all gathered together in the outer deck in the front of the boat, sitting on white plastic chairs, watching the world go by.

I moved from girl to girl, visiting, remembering, complimenting them, studying them, just letting the day float by like the dark water passing by the boat. When I came to Steve and Chris, I did all that, but it wasn't the same, not for me.

I listened to the answers they gave to my questions, but like some old song I couldn't get out of my head I thought, ruefully: *Oh, Christine...where did you go?*

The guys were all very courtly, as always, looking after the girls... Cokes, anyone?...and I remember buying a round of drinks and offering my floppy hat to any of the girls that were now baking in the hot sun. No takers, but they appreciated the offer.

That whole courtesy thing: holding doors open for girls, pulling out their chairs, grabbing checks (when possible) at restaurants, holding their arms, and their coats, when walking down the street— always with the guy on the curb side, in case a car raced by and might splash dirty water on their dresses—well, I just loved it. It was the veneer of civilization to me. It didn't diminish the girls to be the recipient of these gestures of civility. It just had the quality of an old waltz to me. It made everything easier, all the way around, and you never know...maybe a warm kiss would be waiting for you later that night.

After the boat ride ended and we were back on the concrete of Chicago's streets, we walked under a lovely little fountain nestled by the river, that I knew about, but most of the rest of them didn't. Small, charming and just right for the moment, to stand there and let the foamy, falling water all around us make soothing music in our ears.

Then, toward evening, we broke into groups, people going with whoever had cars and went north to exotic Skokie, Illinois to meet at a Middle Eastern restaurant. It was a mile from where I worked for fifteen years, but of course, I had never eaten there. Rick had picked it out. How did he know about it?

I ended up driving alone, but my car was crowded with plenty of thoughts, so it was just as well. I didn't really want to talk to anyone for a while. The day was growing older and soon it would be over, everyone dispersing, again. I didn't want that.

Not yet.

The restaurant, La Baraka, was on a small island of asphalt, with parking all around it. As the assorted members of our happy crew

reassembled inside the place, it was like we were being transported to some faraway land, with wonderful and unfamiliar fragrances drifting from nose to nose, saying,

"Come in, come in…just **wait** 'til you see how I taste!"

After a close examination of the menu to make sure I didn't order anything I was allergic to, which regrettably excluded much of the natural world, and then politely flirting with the (very) lovely waitresses, who spoke in Arabic-accented French, I decided that the restaurant was Lebanese.

It's perplexing to me that the spicy and sensuous menus of Greek, Israeli, Turkish and other Middle-Eastern restaurants have so much in common, but *outside* of the restaurants, the people of some of these same countries always seem to have so much to fight about. When we were all there, it was a roomful of Catholics, Jews, Muslims…maybe a token Protestant…and none of us gave a damn.

It's just a thought, but perhaps the whole UN thing ought to be scrapped and replaced by this enormous floating restaurant anchored in the center of the Mediterranean Sea. They could call it: "The Palace of Lemons, Olives and Sand." Or something else universally appealing to the senses. Everyone would have to check their guns at the door and then see what regional problems they could all work out over tables laden with grape leaves, braised lamb, green peppers, baklava, Turkish coffee and sweet Israeli chocolate liqueurs.

It certainly couldn't be any worse than what's happening over there today, and it would definitely *taste* better. Maybe some of those difficult diplomats would see how easy it is to become friendly over a really good meal. It's not so easy to be intolerant of people that you're belching with, after too many dishes of this and that…and maybe, that.

Which is exactly what we all had that evening, as we ate such wonderfully spicy foods, with lush desserts and very good coffee. People hopped from chair to chair around the long table set up for all of us, endlessly rearranging themselves, as I took candid photographs, many happy photographs of comfortable old friends.

As I circled the table, I backed up to be less obtrusive and to see the people as they really were, without me distracting them. Then I saw Chris, Steve and Rick huddled together, laughing and happy, relaxed, when...

There! Just for a *second*, the light just right, the moment perfect...

I'll never know, man...but I saw Chris smiling her beautiful smile, in profile, and like a rocket through time, I saw her as she was so long ago, as I needed her to be, as she always would be—my...*Cinderella!*

I lowered my camera...to savor the moment, to bask in the warmth of how good it made me feel to see what I saw, like a gift I might never get to see again.

Too soon, it was time for all of us to leave. We all hugged and kissed, traded numbers and made all those promises to call, promises rarely kept. One second, here were all these people I knew huddled together in the dark, outside of the restaurant. Then everyone simply evaporated into the night, like hot desert winds erasing all of our foot prints in the sand.

But I still felt the tingle of magic, from that one clock-stopping moment. I shook hands with all the men, hugged and kissed all the girls, but when I got to Christine, I held onto her for maybe just a *second* longer, not so that she'd notice, but long enough to help me remember this wonderful night.

But then, who can possibly know what our futures will hold?

Thank God for that.

And time went by, but...only just a little bit, it seems to me now...

****

In the afternoon of Monday, March 13, 2006, I was working at my back-issue magazine store, Magazine Memories. It was a quiet day, one of far too many quiet days, when I remembered to turn on my computer to check my e-mail messages for any possible sales. The computer had been off since Saturday night, when I closed, and I was gone on Sunday, so this was the first opportunity for me to catch up with the over one hundred messages, ninety-eight percent of which were junk, spam, whatever. I rapidly deleted them, hoping for at least one meaningful message, when four words caught my attention. It said, simply, terribly,

"Services for Christine Shoub"

I stared at it, truly dumbstruck...stunned.

Then, to my surprise, I suddenly bent over in my chair, like I had been sucker-punched in my gut. My head was on my knees and I was unwilling to sit up, to read those words, to open the message. I was in terrible pain, my face frozen in a grimace.

I could only think, over and over,

"No, no, no, no, no, no...!"

After a while, I turned off the computer, then all the lights, closed up my store hours too early and drove nowhere, anywhere, for a long time. Sometimes...I slowed down the car, rolled over next to a curb, and lowered my head onto the steering wheel, closing my eyes, refusing to think.

The next day, I opened the store, turned on the lights, then the computer and scrolled down the messages, skipping Christine's, and deleting dozens of others. I let the day pass, waited on people, sold magazines, and answered phone calls, while a persistent voice in the back of my head said, over and over, a thousand times:

> *If I don't open the e-mail, then she's not dead. If I don't open the e-mail, then she's not dead. If I don't open the e-mail, then she's not dead. If I don't...*

This went on for three days. Then I steeled myself to read it, and Steve's message said, in part,

"I used e-mail addresses I found among Chris' things. Please let all the others know of this terrible situation.

On Friday, March 10, my wife, Christine ZumBahlen Shoub, died as a result of a motorcycle accident that afternoon. No other vehicles were involved. I donated her organs. She was wearing a helmet, but she suffered fatal head injuries anyway...she survived two hours..."

I read the rest and was uncomprehending of the facts on the page. So I simply returned to my life, and did all the things that I always did. Weeks passed.

Until, on a Monday, March 27, at 5:30 p.m., at the end of another quiet day, the store's door chimes rang and a man I'd met a year before came into my store. He was a young rabbi. Rabbi Douglas

Zeldan.

He had a local cable program, and had asked me the previous year if he could do a story on my very unusual and disappearing kind of business. I met him in my synagogue where I was giving a live reading from my first published book of autobiographical stories. He was there, so I gave one book to him, hoping he would interview me on his show and help me become better known as an author, instead of a store-owner.

I was sick of my store, after sixteen years, seemingly imprisoned by it and I wanted to change my life, but the Rabbi wanted to publicize my past, and I wanted to publicize my future. So there was an impasse.

Then, in a classic Rabbinic decision, he showed up unannounced, with his portable movie camera ready, and said he'd like to do a program on **both** my store and also my book. Out of respect for the man as a Rabbi, and his amazingly simple solution to my stubbornness, I consented, and he started in immediately, that evening.

Going back and forth between the store and my stories, he nimbly accomplished his purposed as I inundated him with anecdotes. No customers interrupted us. After two solid hours, Rabbi Doug was wrapping things up, and he asked me to see if I could briefly sum up the message in my books (there were two by then).

I thought for a moment and then said, looking into the lens of his camera,

"My stories are about character, friendship, loyalty, what friendship really means…that it can be dangerous to be a real friend because one day, your friend may call you…because he's in trouble and needs you *right* now. Maybe you'll get hurt. Real friends accept that risk. A relationship with depth is not just for the 'good' times. I don't think many people understand the concept of friendship so well, anymore…"

Then, pausing to collect my thoughts, seeking an example, I seized on Christine as the best one I could come up with.

Why?

I…don't know why.

I continued.

"I had this friend, Christine…I took her to my Senior Prom in 1968. I just found out she was killed…and…"

And I burst into tears, on camera, covering my face with my hands, feeling so exposed, so embarrassed…and still not understanding where all this pain came from.

Why?

I hardly knew her...I was just on the periphery of her life, just a blip.

Why do I care so much?

****

The Rabbi, who captured all of this on film, stopped to ask me what was wrong. Was I all right?...but I had collected myself, calmed myself—whatever those words mean—and I said I thought he had enough, didn't he? He agreed, whether that was true or not, but he knew when it was time to go. Rabbis ought to know stuff like that...

I accepted what I felt was very real, very true, and called Steve Shoub in Florida to comfort him, to say he could call me if he needed to talk to someone. After all, we're almost related because of my dad, his uncle, the old West Side...

I paused in my rush of words, realizing I was comforting myself, that I could do more, that Christine deserved more...than a paragraph in some old newspaper...I was a writer, wasn't I? Well then, I should do what I can do and give her...give Steve... this...this extra time, this extended reflection, this...something I must do...

I asked Steve some questions, asked him to fill in dates and other information I simply couldn't have known, so that I could write something coherent, something very honest and real. I asked him for his blessing because she was his, and not mine.

He told me to go ahead, and I am so grateful for that, Steve.

But, man...

If some guy had said to me,

"Well, what can you say, as little as you knew her...?"

I would have just stared at him, not having a clue that six weeks after the sudden death of Christine Shoub, I would end up with over ...9,000 words...23 pages....so, really, what more is there for me to say?

For Steve, for Rick, for...me, for her, for all the friends of Chris... just this:

There are all kinds of beautiful.

There's the most obvious physical beauty where a woman is so incredibly and compellingly assembled, it's like she's been kissed by God...

There's the beauty of seeing two people grow old, together, who've been joined by a lifetime of love, pain, victory, loss and a forged determination to care for each other while either still has a breath left in them...

There is the beauty of friendship, real friendship, when a person feels the world closing in on them...and they are lost...and they reach for a phone and call to hear a voice they need...to have something to hold onto...to know they're being really listened to by a kindred soul who isn't charging them by the hour to hear their anguish...someone who will stop whatever they are doing to make a space in their heart for their friend to find some refuge...

There's hearing an unforgettable aria; seeing a movie or a play that is so fresh and real and moving; getting lost in a book that can transport you across oceans or universes by the clarity and originality of the author's thoughts, captured on paper...and then rushing to share the experience with another someone that they care for, so that they can share the wonder of art together, unselfishly, because it matters that the other person might be as enthralled as the person who felt or saw it first, and the other person is worth giving them the chance to discover that same exquisite, creative beauty...

There's being conscious of the planet, wanting all that is good to stay that way after one is gone, so others can see the same unmarred marvels of nature: oceans of trees, canyons, waterfalls, shimmering wetlands filled with myriads of birds, rushing, raging rivers, quiet meadows, clear skies, pristine coastlands, delicious water, herds of buffalo running free...and spending part of one's time, money, and energy to keep things that way...

Then there's that rare someone, who thinks beyond their own mortality, about some other person that they'll never know, never meet. Someone who thinks, like the childhood prayer: If I should die before I wake...maybe my heart will give more life to another who needs a new one, maybe my eyes will let someone see what they've never seen, maybe my kidneys may free someone whose own have failed, and they can escape from the prison of dialysis, and on, and on, leaving behind gifts whose value cannot be measured in gold...

****

I've written so much about someone I never dreamed I would write about, someone who's death churned up powerful feelings, decades-old memories, and a torrent of words that I didn't know were trapped within me, about dear Christine.

Did I...*love* Chris?
Well...

Not like my friend Rick Munden may have, when they were a couple, back in the Sixties. But seventeen year-old guys don't ask each other questions like that. It wouldn't surprise me if that were so. Rick would have seen all that I saw, in Christine.

Not like her life's partner of over thirty-five years, Steve Shoub, surely did. His pain at her loss was so palpable that it made Chris spring back to life for me, like a cloud of memories so demanding, I could not make them disperse. When I last saw them, together, I had no doubt that destiny had joined two people who belonged that way. I was both glad for them...and for her.

How *should* I feel about a very young girl who appeared in my life at two desperate moments, unasked, when I felt hopeless, unwanted, and terrified of my future? When I thought my ugly scars would drive any girl away from me, when I thought no one would ever see past them to want to know the man inside?

How *should* I feel about her wondrous gift to me of her time, her caring, her generosity, her ancient wisdom in a perfect young face that made me feel valuable, wanted, necessary and even, irrationally at the time, attractive?

How *should...*?

How...?

Oh, Jesus Christ...

Christine!

Why'd you have to go and die that way?

I guess —

There is a time to fight

And

There's a time to surrender

To the truth

For me, *that* time

Is now

Yes

I loved you

I just never told you

Christine...

Damn it, Chris...

You...were *all* kinds of beautiful!

Goodbye

My Cinderella

Forever.

Christine ZumBahlen Shoub
1952 - 2006

For Any Author that Chooses to Self-Publish

If you like the physical appearance and quality of my book, then I recommend you contact my printer. He did *not* ask me to tell anyone to do this!

Of all the printers that I interviewed to seek their assistance in publishing my first book, I found **3X Printing** to be the most responsive, the most interested in my goals and the most willing to work with me financially to enable my ambitions to be realized. They made the impossible...possible.

But you can decide for yourself if they are the right printer for your book. I believe in reciprocity. If a person goes out of his way to help me, I believe I should do the same for him.. It helps me sleep better.

Here is their current contact information:

3X Printing
7407 N. Milwaukee Ave.
Niles, IL 60714

Todd Watkins, Owner

Phone: 847-410-0700
Fax: 847-410-0800
email: todd@3xprinting.com

If you enjoyed Volume III of Bob Katzman's tales of adversity, resistance and unknown Chicago history, then it's likely that you will also want to read Volume I:

Fighting Words:
1965 - 1985 Chicago's Bob's Newsstand
I'm Not Dead...*Yet*
Stories of My Life, Volume I

In its pages, you will meet an unexpected group of decent and evil people in unusual situations:

~ An old, bald, one-armed, one-legged angry newsstand mentor seeking a willing apprentice for all his ancient street-wise knowledge...fifteen-year-old me

~ A very shy, silent girl who let me share a last dance with her and rested her head on my shoulder

~ A cranky, tough old woman with a hankering for silver Kennedy half-dollars

~ A major Chicago Mafioso who briefly changed from a 'robbin' hood' to a Robin Hood and saved my giant Downtown newsstand from the bad guys

~ The night shift guy in the hospital, with an attitude, who thought he had my number...but didn't

~ A tough punk who left me bleeding on the playground, laughed and thought it was over...but it wasn't

~ A small, but very tough kid, who saved my ass when there was no one else with the courage to stand by me

~ A raging snowstorm, a beautiful girl, a million kisses, who left me with nothing...but snowflakes

~ Why I thought all sports were stupid, and a patient father who had the wisdom to teach me otherwise

Preview the table of contents on the next page

Fighting Words:
1965 - 1985 Chicago's Bob's Newsstand
I'm Not Dead...*Yet*
Stories of My Life, Volume I

Table of Contents

Why Read My Stories?
Everyone Needs Heroes...Here Are Some of Mine
Introduction: Jewish Geography

1. The Ancient Master of Newsstands: One-Armed Bill
2. And She Said, "He Has Such Beautiful Eyes."
3. Catherine Evans
4. The Mystery of Peter Levy
5. Caldwell Vigilante
6. New Kid at the Private School
7. Picked Last
8. Snowflakes
9. Geneva, Your Lank, Black Hair–It Stirs Me Still
10. Loyalty, Corruption and the Chicago Machine
11. Incident Over Twelve Naked Women, and
     The Red-Hot Biker Chick
12. On Beating a Child
13. Flowers for the Godfather
14. Flowers for the Godfather, Part II or
     The Other Shoe Drops
15. Pain Pill–I Tried to be Nice
16. Tears at the Kitchen Sink
17. My Thoughts on Judaism
         One Man's Jewish Manifesto
         Bar Mitzvah Toast
         Remember the Maccabees

Fighting Words: Escaping and Embracing the Cops of Chicago
Stories of My Life, Volume II

Table of contents

Why Read My Stories?
Everyone Needs Heroes

1. Choices:
   Part I: Escaping and Embracing the Cops of Chicago
   Part II: Mayor Richard J. Daley and My Dog Mike
   Part III: The 1968 Democratic National Convention
   Part IV: My Final Choice
2. From Midnight to Hyde Park...I Escape the Terror
3. Am I My Sister's Keeper?
4. Over the River and Through the Woods, to
   Grandmother's House...in Fargo, North Dakota
5. Don't Ever Underestimate the Quiet Man...
   Tales of My White Knight: Michael Berke
6. Attacked by Ten Thousand Penguins
7. Hiroshi Hamasaki
8. The Tax Man with a Soul
9. Incident at Nick's Diner
10. Some Would Say, One's Enough
11. Annie: Southern Belle in a Neon Hell
12. Brace Yourself
13. Brace Yourself, Part II: The Inevitable Irony
14. Just One More Favor for the Bride-to-Be
15. Five Poems About a Loving Family
    Why Should I Care?
    Parent, Forgive Yourself
    Husband's Lament
    The Meaning of My Little Girl
    Empty Nest

Fighting Words:
1965 - 1985 Chicago's Bob's Newsstand
I'm Not Dead...*Yet*
Stories of My Life, Volume I

Table of Contents

Why Read My Stories?
Everyone Needs Heroes...Here Are Some of Mine
Introduction: Jewish Geography

1.   The Ancient Master of Newsstands: One-Armed Bill
2.   And She Said, "He Has Such Beautiful Eyes."
3.   Catherine Evans
4.   The Mystery of Peter Levy
5.   Caldwell Vigilante
6.   New Kid at the Private School
7.   Picked Last
8.   Snowflakes
9.   Geneva, Your Lank, Black Hair–It Stirs Me Still
10. Loyalty, Corruption and the Chicago Machine
11. Incident Over Twelve Naked Women, and
         The Red-Hot Biker Chick
12. On Beating a Child
13. Flowers for the Godfather
14. Flowers for the Godfather, Part II or
         The Other Shoe Drops
15. Pain Pill–I Tried to be Nice
16. Tears at the Kitchen Sink
17. My Thoughts on Judaism
         One Man's Jewish Manifesto
         Bar Mitzvah Toast
         Remember the Maccabees

If you enjoyed Volume III of Bob Katzman's tales of adversity, resistance and unknown Chicago history, then it's likely that you will also want to read Volume II:

Fighting Words:
Escaping and Embracing the Cops of Chicago

In its pages, you will meet an unexpected group of decent and evil people in unusual situations:

~ A complicated relationship that began with a fourteen year-old boy delivering a prescription to a world-famous author, in 1964, and how their lives periodically intersected for the next thirteen years; a kosher deli opened by Bob at age nineteen; and a burning 1970 newsstand that still lives on today, thirty-five years later.

~ An eighty-eight year old newsstand on Chicago's Northwest Side, the men who run it, the harsh lives they lead and their misunderstood place in a modern society that doesn't grasp their essential value.

~ Revenge, so sweet, between a harassed student who attended but couldn't afford America's premier private high school, and the giant University of Chicago's tuition office, that wasn't adequately prepared for their almost-an-alumni's final exam. Revenge served so sweetly it could make an overbearing manager...explode!

~ A sadistic overnight camp counselor meets his match when he attempts to bully an intractable nine-year-old, and the young boy's unexpected black "fairy godmother" who gives him a lesson about how to cope with impossible situations and people, when a bowl or rich chocolate frosting gradually convinces the boy to listen to her loving wisdom.

~ A wise Rabbi, an unwanted request, a terrible experience of wartime extermination remembered, understood and then shared with others who understood the horror. And a strong faith in what will always be.

~ Friendship. No compromise. Friendship. No confusion. Friendship, unending and secure. So simple an idea, yet some people never get it.

~ A house lost, a spirit shattered. A mysterious dog. Hope, despair, resignation, resolution, a newfound determination to reclaim what was lost, a victory, a Castle, A Dragon, a child, replanted trees, replanted hope, a stubborn Norwegian, a compromise, a smile, and a seduction.

~ A friend dies too young. A memory of extraordinary compassion and kindness. A eulogy on beauty. An anguished cry of pain. A long suppressed love, stubbornly realized. A final farewell. Acceptance.